The
Causes
of
Corruption
of the
Traditional Text
of the
New Testament

The
Causes
of
Corruption
of the
Traditional Text
of the
New Testament

Dean John W. Burgon

Sovereign Grace Publishers, Inc.
P.O. Box 4998
Lafayette, IN 47903

Printed In the United States of America
By Lightning Source, Inc.

Table of Contents

PUBLISHER'S PREFACE

The Causes of the Corruption of the Traditional Text of the Gospels is reproduced from Dean John W. Burgon's book, *The Traditional Text of the Gospels*. It is also included in our title, *Unholy Hands on the Bible*, Volume I, now in its third printing. Many readers of this volume have desired a reprint of this powerful expose of the multitude of errors which are embedded in the modern day versions. It is for this reason that this low-priced paperback is being produced, that the defenders of the inerrancy of the Scriptures may have an affordable book to give away.

WHAT YOU WILL FIND IN THIS FACT-FILLED BOOK

1. Before your eyes, you will see how some errors originated.
2. Dozens of examples demonstrate the unreliability of the Egyptian manuscripts (on which the NA/UBS Greek and nearly all modern versions depend,) with their contradictions, absurdities, scientific impossibilities, and other errors inserted into their "Holy Bible."
3. You will see how fictitious characters happen to be inserted.
4. You will see how a sleepy Egyptian scribe skipped a line, or even two, because the lines ended in the same Greek letters.
5. Causes of scriptural words being deleted, or bracketed by textual critics are explained, to their shame.
6. Corruption of the Lord's Prayer (by deleting doxology in the last words of it) is fully exposed by a simple explanation. These words appear in more than 2,000 manuscripts, are missing from only nine manuscripts. Burgon asks, How did they get into in all those mss.?
7. Burgon explains why it is absurd for the New Versions to convict Matthew and Mark of ignorance of the Old Testament in Matthew 1:7, 10; Mark 1:2. (Mark did *not* put Malachi's words into Isaiah!)
8. How did some words get added to the manuscripts, especially those created in Egypt? Many examples are given to explain these.
9. Why was it the principal aim of the heretics to deny that Jesus Christ is co-equal God in the Trinity? Find the answer here.
10. How did it happen that the modern versions have the God-man bound to earth, rather than to be in Heaven at the same time? p. 99.
No such precise, helpful explanations can be found anywhere else!

Jay P. Green, Sr., Publisher

THE CAUSES OF THE CORRUPTION OF THE TRADITIONAL TEXT OF THE HOLY GOSPELS

INTRODUCTION

In the companion volume to this, the Traditional Text, that is, the Text of the Gospels which is the resultant of all the evidence faithfully and exhaustively presented and estimated according to the best procedure of the courts of law, has been traced back to the earliest ages in the existence of those sacred writings.

On the one hand it has been shown that the Traditional Text must be found, not in a mere transcript, but in a laborious revision of the Received Text. And on the other hand it must be recognized that this Traditional Text will differ but slightly from the Received Text, which has been generally received during the last two and a half centuries.

The strength of the position of the Traditional Text lies in its being logically deducible from all the varied evidence when it has been sifted, proved, passed, weighed, compared, compounded and contrasted with the testimony of those who dissent to it. The contrast is indeed great in almost all instances upon which controversy has gathered. On the one side the vast mass of authorities is assembled; on the other side stands a small group. There is a considerable advantage to this small group due to the fact that numerous students refuse to look beneath the surface after deciding that the general witness is in their favor borne by the two oldest MSS. of the Gospels. That advantage however shrinks into nothing under the light of rigid examination. The claim for the Text in these two oldest MSS., which were penned in the Semi-Arian period, was rejected when Semi-Arianism fell into permanent disfavor. The argument by Dr. Hort and others that the Traditional Text found in the vast majority of manuscripts was a new Text created in the fourth century has been refuted by examination of the quotations of the Fathers in the first four centuries, and by the early Syriac and Latin Versions. Besides, those two manuscripts have been traced to a local source in the library of Caesarea.

It is evident that the turning-point of the controversy between ourselves and the neologian school must lie in the centuries before St. Chrysostom. If the Traditional Text not only gained supremacy at that era, but did not exist in early ages, then our contention is vain. A true Text must go back without break or intermission to the original autographs, because if it ceased through break or intermission it loses the essential feature of genuine tradition. But if it is proved to reach back in unbroken line to the time of the Evangelists, or to a period as near to them as surviving testimony can prove, then the theory of a 'Syrian' text evidently falls to the ground. In the first part of this volume we have proved the continual existence of the Traditional Text is witnessed by the earliest fathers and versions.

In this section the other half of the subject will be discussed. Instead of exploring the genuine Text, we shall treat of the corruptions of it. Here we will track error in its many forms to a few sources and heads. The origination of the pure Text in the inspired writings of the Evangelists will then be vindicated by the evident origin of the deflections from it, as discovered in the natural defects or iniquities of men. Corruption will the more show itself in true colors, and it will not so readily be mistaken for genuineness when the real history is unfolded, and the mistakes accounted for.

It seems clear that corruption of the Text appeared in the very earliest age. As soon as the Gospel was preached, the incapacity of human nature for preserving accuracy must have asserted itself in constant distortion more or less of the sacred stories, as they were told or retold amongst Christians, whether in writing or in oral transmission. Mistakes would inevitably arise from the universal human tendency to mix error with truth. And as soon as inaccuracy had done its baleful work, a spirit of infidelity and of hostility to the essentials and details of Christianity must have impelled those that were either imperfect Christians, or no Christians at all, to corrupt the sacred Gospel. So it appears that errors crept in at the very inception of the Christian religion. The Gospels were certainly not written until some thirty years after the Ascension of Christ. The Gospels would be the authorized versions in their entirety of the stories constituting the life of our Lord. And the corruption must have come into existence *before* the antidote was found in complete documents accepted by the authorities in the Church. If that corruption arose at the very first spread of Christianity, before the record of our Lord's life has assumed permanent shape in the Four Gospels, all is easy to understand. Such corruption, inasmuch as it beset the oral and written stories which were afterward incorporated in the Gospels, would creep into the authorized narrations, and would vitiate them till it was ultimately cast out towards the end of the fourth and in the succeeding centuries.

Starting from the very beginning, and gaining additions in the several ways described in this volume by Dean Burgon, it would possess such vigor as to impress itself on Low-Latin and even the better Latin MSS., on the Diatessaron, the Curetonian and Lewis MSS. of the fifth century, the Codex Bezai (D) of the sixth, and also on the Vatican (**B**) and Sinaitic (**ℵ**) of the fourth century. Later these corruptions may be seen in the Dublin palimpsest of the sixth, the Codex Regius (L) of the eighth, the St. Gall of the ninth, and the Codex Zacynthius of the eighth, and a few others. We admit that the corruptions in these are old, even though the manuscripts enshrining them do not date that far back, and though they cannot always prove their ancestry.

In the following treatise Dean Burgon has divided the causes of corruption under various heads, five discussing those that came about by accident, and 10 those that came about by intentional additions or subtractions by both the enemies of the faith, and by those who counted themselves defenders of the faith. This dissection of the mass of corruption; this classification of the numerous causes which are found to have been at work from time to time, should prove interesting to all. For by revealing the influences at work, it sheds light on the entire controversy. By this the student can see clearly how and why certain passages became corrupted.

CHAPTER 1

GENERAL CORRUPTION: We hear sometimes scholars complain that it is discreditable to us as a Church [Dean Burgon's reference to Church is to the Anglican Church of England, in which he was a dean—Ed.] not to have long since put forth by authority a revised Greek Text of the New Testament. Men who assume that the case of the Scriptures and that of other ancient writings are similar evidently misunderstand the question. For such remonstrances are commonly followed by such statements as these: That the Received Text is that of Erasmus — that it was constructed in haste, and without skill — that it is based on a very few manuscripts, and those bad ones — that it belongs to an age when scarcely any of our present critical helps were available, etc. To listen to these advocates of Revision you would almost suppose that it fared with the Gospel at this instant as it had fared with the original copy of the law for many years until the days of king Josiah (2 Kings 22:8).

Yielding to no one in my desire to see the Greek of the New Testament judiciously revised, I freely avow that recent events have convinced me that we have not among us the men to conduct such an undertaking. Better a thousand times to leave things as they are, than to risk having the stamp of authority set upon an unfortunate revision, such as appeared in 1881, which claims to represent the combined learning of the Church, the chief Sects, and the Socinian [Unitarian] members of the Church.

If these desiring to see the commonly received text revised intend to have it made absolutely faultless actually were calling for the collation of the many copies which have become known to us within the last two centuries, and if they are bent on procuring a re-editing of the ancient Versions; and if they would be delighted that a band of scholars had combined to index every place of Scripture quoted by any of the Fathers — if this were meant, then we would be entirely at one with them. And this would be especially true if we could further gather from the program that a fixed intention was cherished of abiding by the result of such an appeal to all ancient evidence.

Now I am bent on calling attention to certain features of the problem which have very generally escaped attention. It does not seem to be understood that the Scriptures of the New Testament stand on entirely different footing from every other ancient writing which can be named. A few plain remarks ought to bring this fact, for a fact it is, home to every thoughtful person. And the result will be that men will approach the subject with more caution — with doubts and misgivings — with a fixed determination to be on their guard against any form of plausible influence. Then their prejudices will scatter to the winds. At every step they then will insist on proof.

In the first place, then, let it be observed that the New Testament Scriptures are wholly without parallel in respect of their having been so frequently multiplied from the very first. They are by consequence contained at this day in an extravagantly large number of copies [near five thousand]. There is nothing like this, or at all approaching to it, in the case of any secular writing. And the very necessity for multiplying copies — a necessity which has made itself felt in every age and in every part of the world — has resulted in an immense number of variants. Words have been dropped; vowels have been inadvertently confounded by copyists more or less competent; and the meaning of Scripture in countless places has suffered to a surprising degree.

Further, the Scriptures became a mark for the shafts of Satan from the beginning, for the very reason that they were known to be the Word of God. So they were as eagerly solicited by heretical teachers on the one hand, as they were hotly defended by the orthodox on the other. Therefore, from friends and from foes the Scriptures are known to have experienced injury, and that in the earliest age of all. Nothing of the kind can be predicated of any other ancient writings. This consideration alone should suggest a severe exercise of judicial impartiality in the handling of ancient evidence of whatever sort. Observe that I have not said — and I certainly do not mean — that the Scriptures themselves have been permanently corrupted either by friend or foe. Error was fitful and uncertain, and was contradicted by other error. And it eventually sank before a manifold witness to the truth. Nevertheless, certain manuscripts belonging to a few small groups, particular copies of a Version, individual Fathers, these do, to this present hour, bear traces incontestably of ancient mischief.

And this is not nearly all. The fourfold structure of the Gospel has lent itself to a certain kind of licentious handling — of which in other ancient writings we have no experience. One critical owner of a Codex considered himself at liberty to assimilate the narratives; another undertook to correct them in order to bring them into what seemed to himself to be greater harmony. Brevity is found to have been a paramount object with some, and Transposition to have amounted to a passion with others. Conjectural Criticism [still with us today—Ed.] was evidently practiced largely, and with almost as little felicity as when Bentley held the pen. Lastly, there can be no question that there was a certain school of critics who considered themselves competent to improve the style of the Holy Ghost throughout. And before the members of the Church had gained a familiar acquaintance with the words of the New Testament, blunders continually crept into the text of individual manuscripts, of more or less heinous importance. All this, which was chiefly done during the second and third centuries, introduces an element of difficulty in the handling of ancient evidence which can never be safely neglected. This should make a thoughtful man suspicious of every various reading which comes in his way, especially if it is attended with but slender attestation. As shown in the first part of this volume, the names of the Codexes chiefly vitiated in this sort prove to be BℵCDL, and of the versions, the two Coptic, the Curetonian, and certain of the old Latin. of the fathers, Origen, Clement of Alexandria, and to some extent Eusebius must be suspected.

Add to all that goes before the peculiar subject-matter of the New Testament Scriptures, and it will become abundantly plain why they should have been liable to a series of assaults which make it reasonable that they should now at last be approached by ourselves as no other ancient writings are, or can be. The nature of God: His Being and Attributes; the history of Man's Redemption; the soul's eternal destiny; the mysteries of the unseen world — concerning these and every other similar high doctrinal subject, the sacred writings alone speak with a voice of absolute authority. And surely by this time enough has been said to explain why these Scriptures should have been made a battlefield during some centuries, and especially in the fourth century. And having been made the subject of strenuous contention, it is no wonder that copies of the Scriptures should exhibit to this hour traces of those many adverse influences. No other ancient writing knew or could know anything like these causes of depravation. Therefore we must handle the Textual Criticism of the New Testament in an entirely difference spirit from that of any other book.

THE CAUSES OF CORRUPTION OF THE NEW TESTAMENT TEXT

I wish now to investigate the causes of the corruption of the Text of the New Testament. I do *not* entitle this a discussion of *Various Readings* because I consider that expression to be incorrect and misleading. I think it necessary even a second time to call attention to the impropriety which attends the use of that heading. Thus Codex **B** differs from the commonly received Text of Scripture in the Gospels alone in 7578 places, of which no less than 2877 are instances of omission. In fact omissions constitute by far the larger number of what are commonly called *Various Readings*. How then can those be called 'various readings' which are not readings at all? For example, how can that be said to be a 'various reading' of St. Mark 16:9-20 which consists in the circumstance that the last 12 verses are left out by two MSS.? Again, how can it be called a 'various reading' of St. John 21:25 to bring the Gospel abruptly to a close, as Tischendorf does at verse 24? These are really nothing else but indications either of a mutilated or else an interpolated text. The question to be resolved is this: on which side does the corruption lie? Also, how did it originate?

Waiving this, however, the term is objectionable on other grounds. It is to beg the whole question to assume that every irregularity in the text of Scripture is a 'various reading.' The very expression carries with it an assertion of importance. At least it implies a claim to consideration. Because it is termed a 'various reading' it might be thought that a critic is entitled to call into question the commonly received text. But rather it will be found that nine divergences out of ten are of no manner of significance and are thus not entitled to consideration, as every one must see at a glance who will attend to the matter ever so little. *Various Readings* in fact is a term which rightly belongs only to the criticism of the text of profane [secular] authors. This, like many other notions which have been imported from the same region into this department of inquiry, only tends to confuse and perplex the judgment.

No variety in the Text of Scripture can properly be called a *various reading*, when it may be safely declared that it never has been read, nor ever will be as true Scripture. In the case of profane authors, where the MSS. are few, almost every plausible substitution of one word for another, if really entitled to alteration, is looked upon as a various reading of the text. But in the Gospels, the case is far otherwise, the copies being so numerous. There we are able to convince ourselves in a moment that the supposed *various reading* is nothing else but an instance of licentiousness or inattention on the part of a previous scribe or scribes, and we can afford to neglect it accordingly. ["perhaps this point may be cleared by dividing readings into two classes; (1) such as really have strong evidence for their support, and require examination before we can be certain that they are corrupt; and (2) those which afford no doubt as to their being destitute of foundation, and are only interesting as specimens of the modes in which error was sometimes introduced. Evidently the latter class are not *various* at all— Edward Miller.]

This is the point to which I desire to bring the reader and to urge upon his consideration; that the number of *various readings* in the New Testament properly so called has been greatly exaggerated. In reality they are exceedingly few in number. And it is to be expected that as sound (sacred) criticism advances, and principles are established, and conclusions recognized, instead of becoming multiplied, they will become fewer and fewer, and at last will entirely disappear. That only deserves the name of a *Various Reading* which comes to us so respectably recommended as to be entitled to our sincere consideration and respect. Better still it should be of such a kind as to inspire some degree of reasonable suspicion that after all it may prove to be the true way of exhibiting the text.

Therefore, the inquiry on which we are about to engage grows naturally out of the considerations which have been already offered. We propose to ascertain in what way these many strange corruptions of the text have arisen, so far as it is practicable at the end of so many hundred years. Very often we shall only have to inquire how it has come to pass that the text exhibits signs of having been perturbed at a certain place. The disquisitions that follow have no place in reviewing any other text than that of the New Testament, because a few plain principles would suffice to solve every difficulty. The less usual word mistaken for the word of more frequent occurrence — clerical carelessness — a gloss finding its way into the text — such explanations as these would probably in other cases suffice to account for every ascertained corruption of the text. But it is far otherwise here, as I propose to make fully apparent by and by. Various disturbing influences have been at work for a great many years, of which secular productions know absolutely nothing, nor indeed can know.

The importance of such an inquiry will become apparent as we proceed. But it may be convenient to attend to the matter briefly at the outset. It frequently happens that the one remaining plea of many critics for adopting 'readings' of a certain kind is the inexplicable nature of the phenomena which these 'readings' exhibit. The critic will say, "How can you account for such a reading if it is not authentic? Or they will say nothing, leaving it to be inferred that this 'reading' they adopt must be accepted as true, and this in spite of its intrinsic improbability, and inspite of the slender amount of evidence on which it rests. Such critics lose sight of the correlative difficulty, which is, 'How can it be explained that the rest of the copies read the place otherwise? In such cases it is impossible to overestimate the importance of detecting the particular cause which has brought about, or which at least will fully account for, this depravation. Once this is done, it is hardly too much to say that a case presents itself such as when a mask has been torn away, and the ghost is discovered behind it.

IMPORTANT CONSIDERATIONS WHEN EXAMINING THE ERRORS IN VARIOUS NEW TESTAMENT MANUSCRIPTS

When I take into my hands an ancient copy of the Gospels I expect that it will exhibit sundry inaccuracies and imperfections. The discovery creates no uneasiness so long as the phenomena evolved are of a certain kind and range:

1. Whatever belongs to peculiarities of spelling or fashions of writing can be disregarded. For example, it is clearly consistent with perfect good faith for a scribe to spell κράβαττον in several different ways; that he should write οὕω for οὕως, or on the contrary; that he should add or omit what grammarians call ν ἐφελκυστικόν. The questions really touched by irregularities such as these concern the date and country where the MS. was produced; not by any means the honesty or animus of the copyist. The man fell into the method which was natural to him, or which he found prevailing around him. *Itacisms*, therefore, as they are called, of whatever kind — by which is meant the interchange of such vowels and diphthongs as ι-ει, αι-ε, η-οι-υ, ο-ω, η-ει, need excite no uneasiness. it is true

that such variations may occasionally result in very considerable inconvenience. For it will sometimes happen that a different reading is the consequence. But the copyist may have done his work in perfect good faith for all that. It is not he that occasions me perplexity, but the language and the imperfect customs amidst which he wrote.

2. In like manner the reduplication of syllables, words, clauses, sentences, is consistent with entire sincerity of purpose on the part of the copyist. This inaccuracy is to be deplored, since a reduplicated syllable often really affects the sense. But for the most part nothing worse ensures than that the page is disfigured with errata.

3. On the other hand the occasional omission of words, whether few or many — especially that passing from one line to the corresponding place in a subsequent line, which generally results from the proximity of a similar ending — is purely a venial offence. it is an evidence of carelessness, but it proves nothing worse.

4. Further, slight inversions, especially of ordinary words — or the adoption of some more obvious and familiar collocation of particles in a sentence — or the occasional substitution of one common word for another (such as εἶπε for ἔλεγε) need not provoke resentment. It is an indication of nothing worse than slovenliness on the part of the writer or the group or succession of writers.

5. Besides the substitution of one word for another, cases frequently occur where even the introduction into the text of one or more words which cannot be thought to have stood in the original authograph of the Evangelist, need create no offence. It is often possible to account for their presence in a legitimate way.

But it is high time to point out that irregularities which fall under these five heads are only tolerable within narrow limits; they always require careful watching. For they may easily become excessive, or even be seen to betray an animus; and in either case they pass at once into quite a different category. From cases of excusable drowsiness or dullness they degenerate, either into instances of inexcusable licentiousness, or else into cases of downright fraud.

6. Careful observation must be given in case a Codex *(a)* habitually omits entire sentences or significant clauses; *(b)* again and again in the course of the same page seriously tampers with the phraseology of the Evangelist; and, *(c)* inserts interpolations here and there which will not admit of loyal interpretation. in such a case we cannot but learn to regard with habitual distrust the Codex in which all these notes are found combined. It is as when a witness, whom we suspected of nothing worse than a bad memory, or a random tongue, or a lively imagination, at last is convicted of deliberate suppression of parts of his evidence, misrepresentation of facts, etc.; in fact of deliberate falsehood.

7. But now suppose the case of a MS. in which words or clauses are clearly omitted with design; where expressions are withheld which are confessedly harsh or critically difficult; where whole sentences or parts of them are omitted which are known to have controversial bearing. Suppose further that the same MS. abounds in worthless paraphrase, and contains apocryphal additions throughout — then what are we to think of it as our guide? There can be but one opinion on the subject. From habitually trusting, we now must entertain inveterate distrust, for we have ascertained its character. We thought it to be a faithful witness, but now we find from experience of its transgressions that we have fallen into bad company. The witness of that Codex may be false or true, but our confidence in it is at an end.

TWO CLASSES OF CORRUPTION: INADVERTENT, OR BY DESIGN

It may be regarded as certain that most of the aberrations discoverable in Codexes of the Sacred Text have arisen in the first instance from the merest inadvertency of the scribes. That such was the case in a vast number of cases is in fact demonstrable. [Inaccuracy in the apprehension of the Divine Word, which in the earliest ages was imperfectly understood, and ignorance of Greek in primitive Latin translators, were prolific sources of error. The influence of Lectionaries, in which Holy Scripture was cut up into separate Lections, either with or without an introduction, remained with habitual hearers, and led them off in copying to paths which had become familiar. Acquaintance with *harmonies* or *Diatessarons* caused copyists insensibly to assimilate one Gospel to another. And doctrinal predilections, as in the case of those who belonged to the school of Origen, were the source of lapsing into expressions which were not the *verba ipsissima* of Holy Writ. in such cases, when the inadvertency was genuine and was not mingled with any overt design, it is much to be noted that the error seldom propagated itself extensively—Edward Miller.]

But next, well-meant endeavors must have been made at a very early period "to rectify" the text which had been unintentionally corrupted. And thus what began in inadvertence is sometimes found in the end to exhibit traces of design. To cite a favorite example, it is clear to me that in the earliest age (A.D. 100?) some copyist of St. Luke 2:14 (call him X) inadvertently omitted the second *EN* in the Angelic hymn. now if the persons (call them Y and Z) whose business it became in turn to reproduce the early copy which had been inadvertently depraved had both but been content to transcribe exactly what they saw before them, the error of their predecessor (X) would have been speedily detected, remedied, and forgotten. For every one must have seen, as well as Y and Z that it was impossible to translate the sentence which resulted from the error of X: ἐπὶ γῆς εἰρήνη ἀνθρώποις εὐδοκία. Reference would then would have been made to any other copy of the third Gospel, and together with the omitted preposition (ἐν) sense would have been restored to the passage. But unhappily one of the two supposed copists being a learned grammarian who [perhaps] had no other copy at hand to refer to, undertook to force a meaning into the manifestly corrupted text — and he did it by affixing to εὐδοκία the sign of the genitive case (ς). Unhappy effort of misplaced skill! That copy [or those copies] became the immediate progenitor [or progenitors] of a large family — from which the Latin copies are descended — so that by it comes to pass that Latin Christendom sings the Hymn *Gloria in excelsis* incorrectly to the present day. The error committed by the same copyists survives in the four oldest copies of the passage, in **B*** and **א***, A and D; though happily in no others. It is also in the Old Latin, Vulgate and Gothic versions, and only in those of the versions. All the Greek authorities excepting those noted above united in condemning the evident blunder[1].

I once hoped that it might be possible to refer all the corruptions of the Text of Scripture to ordinary causes, such as careless transcription, accidents, misplaced critical assiduity, doctrinal animus, small acts of unpardonable licence, etc. But increased attention and enlarged acquaintance with the subject have convinced me that by far the larger number of the omissions of such Codexes as **א**BLD must be due to quite a different cause. These MSS. omit so many words, phrases, sentences, verses of Scripture, that it is altogether incredible that the proximity of like endings can have much to do with the matter. Inadvertency may be made to bear the blame of some omissions, but it cannot bear the blame of shrewd and significant omissions of clauses which invariably leave the sense complete. A systematic and perpetual mutilation of the inspired Text must be the result of design, not of accident.

CHAPTER 1 FOOTNOTES

Page 8: 'I am inclined to believe that in the age immediately succeeding that of the Apostles, some person or persons of great influence and authority executed a Revision of the N.T. and gave the world the result of such labors in a 'correct Text.' The guiding principle seems to have been to seek to *abridge* the Text, to lop off whatever seemed redundant, or which might in any way be spared, and to eliminate from one Gospel whatever expressions occurred elsewhere in another Gospel. Clauses which slightly obscured the speaker's meaning; or which seemed to hang loose at the end of a sentence; or which introduced a consideration of difficulty — words which interfered with the easy flow of a sentence — everything of this kind such a personage seems to have held himself free to discard. But what is more serious, passages which occasioned some difficulty, as in the case of the woman taken in adultery; physical perplexity, as the troubling of the water; spiritual revulsion, as the agony in the garden — all these the reviser or revisers seemed to have judged it safest simply to eliminate. It is difficult to understand how any persons in their senses could have so acted by the sacred deposit. But it does not seem improbable that at some very remote period there were found some who did act in some such way. Let it be observed, however, that unlike some critics I do not base any real argument upon what appears to me to be a not unlikely supposition.

CHAPTER 2

ACCIDENTAL CAUSES OF CORRUPTION
I. PURE ACCIDENT

[It often happens that more causes than one are combined in the origin of the corruption in any one passage. In the following history of a blunder and of the fatal consequences that ensured, only the first step was accidental. But much instruction may be derived from the initial blunder, and though the later stages in the history come under another head, they nevertheless illustrate the effects of early accident, besides throwing light on parts of the discussion which are yet to come.]

FIRST EXAMPLE

We are sometimes able to trace the origin and progress of accidental depravations of the text. Attend to what is found in St. John 10:29. There, instead of *"My Father, who has given them* [viz. *My sheep] to Me, is greater than all "* — Tischendorf, Tregelles, Alford, [and many modern 'translators'] are for reading, 'That thing which My (or the) Father has given to Me is greater (i.e. is a greater thing) than all.' This is a vastly different proposition, and, whatever it may mean, it is wholly inadmissable there, as the context proves. This is the result of sheer accident in the beginning:

St. John certainly wrote the familiar words; ὁ πατήρμον ὅς δέδωκέ μοι, μείζων πάντων ἐστί. But with the licentiousness [or inaccuracy] which prevailed in the earliest age, some remote copyist is found to have substituted for ὅς δέδωκέ its grammatical equivalent, ὁ δεδωκώς. And this proved fatal, for it was only necessary for another scribe to substitute μεῖζον for μείζων (after the example of such places as S. Matt. 12:6,41,42, etc.), and thus the door had been opened to at least four distinct deflections from the evangelical verity, and these straightway found their way into manuscripts:

(1) ο δεδωκως . . . μειζων, which survives only in D.
(2) ος δεδωκε . . . μειζον, which survives only in AX.
(3) ο δεδωκε . . . μειζων, which is only found in אl.
(4) ο δεδωκε . . . μειζον, which is the peculiar property of B.

The first and second of these sufficiently represent the Evangelist's meaning, though neither of them is what he actually wrote. But the third is untranslatable, and the fourth is nothing else but a desperate attempt to force a meaning into the third by writing μειζον for μειζων; thus treating ο not as the article but as the neuter of the relative ὅς.

This last exhibition of the text, which in fact scarcely yields an intelligible meaning and rests on the minimum of manuscript evidence, would long since have been forgotten, but that it was executed from MSS. of the same vicious type as Cod. B. [See the passages quoted in Scrivener's introduction, ii. 270-2, 4th edition.] Accordingly, all the Latin copies, and therefore all the Latin Fathers follow it. Characteristically Westerns resolutely extracted a meaning from whatever they presumed to be genuine Scripture, and one can but admire the piety which insists on finding sound Divinity in what proves after all to be nothing else but a sorry blunder. The Greeks knew better. Basil, Chrysostom, Cyril on nine occasions, Theodoret — as many as quote the place —

invariably exhibit the Received Text (ὅς ...μεῖζων)which is obviously the true reading and may on no account suffer molestation.

But one may ask, "Although Patristic and manuscript evidence are lacking for the reading of **B**, is it not a significant circumstance that three translations of such high antiquity as the Latin, the Bohairic and the Gothic should concur in supporting it? And does it not inspire extraordinary confidence in **B** to find that **B** alone of MSS. agrees with them?" I answer: It makes me more and more distrustful of the Latin, the Bohairic and the Gothic versions to find them exclusively siding with **B** on such an occasion as this. it is obviously not more significant that these three conspire with **B**, than that the Syriac, the Sahidic and the Ethiopic should here combine against **B**. On the other hand, how utterly insignificant is the testimony of **B** when opposed to *all* the other uncials, all the cursives, and all the Greek fathers who quote the place. So far from inspiring me with confidence in **B**, the present indication of the fatal sympathy of that Codex with the corrupt copies from which confessedly many of the Old Latin were executed, confirms me in my habitual distrust of **B**. About the true reading of St. John 10:29, there really exists no manner of doubt. As for the 'old uncials' they are (as usual) hopelessly at variance on the subject. In an easy sentence of only nine words — which Tischendorf exhibits in conformity with *no* known Codex, while Tregelles and Alford blindly follow Cod. **B** — they have contrived to invent *five* 'various readings'. Shall we wonder more at the badness of the Codexes to which we are now invited to pin our faith; or shall we wonder at the infatuation of these guides?

CLERICAL ERRORS

Sufficient attention has not been paid to grave disturbances of the Text which have resulted from a slight clerical error. Once trace a serious Textual disturbance back to what for convenience may be called a 'clerical error,' and you are supplied with an effectual answer to a form of inquiry which otherwise is sometimes very perplexing. If the true meaning of a passage be what you suppose, for what conceivable reason should the scribe have misrepresented it in this strange way; in short having made nonsense of the place? it is always interesting, and sometimes instructive, to note what has been its subsequent history and progress.

Some specimens of the thing referred to have been given elsewhere. A mistake dating from the second and third centuries has remained without a patron all down the subsequent ages, until at last it has been suddenly taken up in our own times and straightway palmed off on an unlearned generation as the genuine work of the Holy Spirit. Whereas the Church has until now supposed that S. Paul's company *"were in all in the ship two hundred threescore and sixteen souls "* (Acts 27:37), Drs. Westcott and Hort, relying on the authority of **B** and the Sahidic Version, insist that what S. Luke wrote was *about seventy six*. What can have given rise to such a discrepancy? We answer, It was a mere accident. First, whereas S. Luke certainly wrote ἦμεν δὲ ἐν τῷ πλοίς αἱ πᾶσαι ψυχαί, his last six words at some very early period underwent the familiar process of Transposition, and it became, αἱ πᾶσαι ψυχαὶ ἐν τῷ πλοίς; whereby the word πλοίς and the *numbers* διακόσιαι ἑβδομηκονταέξ were brought into close proximity — it is thus that Lachmann, Tischendorf, Tregelles, etc. exhibit the place. But since 276 when represented in Greek numerals is coϛ, the inevitable consequence was that the words written in uncials ran thus; ΨΥΑΙΕΝΤΩΠΛΟΙΩΨΟ. Behold the secret is out! There has been no intentional falsification of the text, no critical disinclination to believe that a "corn-ship, presumably heavy-laden would contain so many souls." The discrepancy has been the result of sheer accident, it is the merest blunder. Some second-century copyist connected the last letter of ΠΛΟΙΩ with the next ensuring number Ω, which stands for 200, and has made an independent word of it by writing ὡς —that is, *about seventy six*. His blunder would have been diverting if confined merely to a codex which is full of blunders. But when it is adopted by Westcott and Hort, and by their influence has been foisted into the margin of the English Revised Version, it becomes high time that we should declaim against such a gratuitous depravation of Scripture.

All this ought not to have required explaining, the blunder being so gross and its history so obvious. But even if its origin had been ever so obscure, the most elementary critical knowledge joined to a little mother-wit ought to convince a man that the reading in **B** cannot be trustworthy. Although a man might say 'about seventy,' or 'about eighty' (as Epiphaius quotes the place) who cannot see that 'about seventy-six' is an impossible expression? A reading discoverable *only* in Cod. **B** and one Egyptian version may always be dismissed as certainly spurious. But lastly, these two witnesses give divergent testimony, for the Sahidic version arranges the words in an order peculiar to itself.

ANOTHER CORRUPTION: Acts 18:7

Another corruption of the text originating in sheer accident occurs in Acts 18:7. It is related concerning S. Paul, at Corinth, that having left the synagogue of the Jews, *"he entered into a certain man's house named Justus"* (ὀνόματι Ἰούστου). That this is what S. Luke wrote is to be inferred from the fact that it is found in almost every known copy of the Acts, beginning with A D G H L P. Chrysostom — the only Greek Father who quotes the place — so quotes it. But the last syllable of *name* (ONOMATI) and the first three letters of *Justus* (IOY) in an uncial copy may easily get mistaken for an independent word. It only lacks a horizontal stroke at the top of the second ι in TIIOY to produce *Titus* (TITOYO. Accordingly in the Syriac and Sahidic versions *Titus* actually stands *in place of Justus* — a reading no longer found in any extant Greek codex. As a matter of fact the error did not result in the substitution of *Titus* for *Justus*, but in the introduction of *both* names where S. Luke wrote only one. ℵ and E, the Vulgate, and the Coptic version exhibit *Titus Justus*. And that this is a true account of the birth and parentage of *Titus* is proved by the tell-tale circumstance that in **B** the letters TI and IOY are all religiously retained, and a supernumery letter (T) has been thrust in between — and the result is one more imaginary gentleman, viz. *Titius Justus* — he is found *nowhere else* but in codex **B**. [Yet this "imaginary foreigner has been advanced to citizenship and assigned a local habitation and a name" by the English revisers, and by some critics and translators since those days when the men in the "Jerusalem Chamber" had their wondrously drowsy days and allowed such manipulations of the inspired text to be foisted upon them.]

But for a far sadder travesty of sacred words, the reader is referred to what has happened in S. Matt. 11:23 and S. Luke 10:15, where our Saviour is made to ask an unmeaning question, instead of being permitted to announce a solemn fact concerning Capernaum. The error here is so transparent that the wonder is how it can ever have imposed on anyone. What makes the matter serious is that it gives a turn to a certain Divine saying, of which it is incredible that either our Saviour or his Evangelists knew anything. We have always believed that the

solemn words ran as follows: *"And thou, Capernaum, which art exalted (ἡ . . .*
ὑψωθεῖσα *unto heaven, shalt be brought down (***καταβιβασθήση***) to hell."*
For this our Revisionists invite us to substitute in S. Luke as well as in S.
Matthew: "And thou, Capernaum, shalt thou be exalted (**μὴ . . . ὑψωθήση**)
unto heaven?" And then, in S. Matthew but not in S. Luke, "Thou shalt go down
(**καταβήση**) into Hades." Now what could have happened to occasion such a
curious perversion of our Lord's true utterance, and to cause him to ask an
unmeaning question about the future, when he was clearly announcing a *fact*
founded on the history of the past?

A stupid blunder has been made, of which traces survive, as usual, only in the
same little handful of suspicious documents. The final letter of Capernaum (**M**)
by cleaving to the next ensuing letter (**H**) has been made into an independent
word (**MH**); and this new word then necessitates a change in the construction,
causing the sentence to become interrogative. And yet fourteen of the uncial
MSS. and the whole body of the cursives know nothing of this. Nor does the
Peschito Version, nor the Gothic Version. nor does Chrysostom, Cyril, nor ps.-
Caesarius, nor Theodoret, these being the only Fathers who quote either place.
The sole witnesses for this corruption (**μὴ . . . ὑψωθήση**) in both Matthew and
Luke are **ℵ**, **B**, copies of the old Latin, Cureton's Syriac, the Coptic, and the
Ethiopic versions — a consensus of authorities which ought to be held fatal to any
reading. C joins the conspiracy in Matthew, but not in Luke. D and l consent in
Luke, but not in Matthew. The Vulgate sides with **ℵ** and **B** in Matthew, but
forsakes them in Luke. In writing *both* times **καταβήση** (thou shalt go down),
codex **B** is supported by a single manuscript, D, being forsaken this time by **ℵ**.
But because in Matt. 11:23 **B** obtains the sanction of the Latin copies,
καταβήση is actually introduced into the Revised Text [and into the Nestle
and U.B.S texts, following them in English translations by those using those texts
— the NIV, Marshall's interlinear, etc.— Ed.]. And though footnotes hint that
there are other ancient authorities which read *"shall be brought down,"* they do
not make the reader aware of the fact that there are really only *two manuscripts
in existence that read anything else*! And those two manuscripts are convicted of
having *borrowed their quotation from the Septuagint* (Isaiah 14:15), and
therefore stand self-condemned. Were all who insist upon reading with **B** and D
καταβήση in both places fast asleep when they became consenting parties to
this sad mistake?

Acts 20:24, A Case of Attraction

There is a case of attraction in Acts 20:24. It is but the change of a single letter
(**λόγου** for **λόγον**), yet that minute deflection from the truth has led to a
complete mangling of perhaps the most affecting of S. Paul's utterances. I refer
to the famous words, *"But none of these things move me, neither count I my
life dear to myself, so that I might finish my course with joy "* — which is thus
excellently, because idiomatically, rendered by our Translators of 1611.

Because someone sustituted **οὐδενὸς λόTOY** for **οὐδενὸς λόTON**
(the accusative after **ποιοῦμαι**), it became necessary for them to find something
else for the verb to govern. **Τὴν ψυχήν** was at hand, but **οὐδὲ ἔχω** stood in the
way, so these words must go; and go they did, as **B**, C, and **ℵ** remain to attest[1]
Τιμίαν should have gone also, if the sentence was to be made translatable, but
Τιμίαν was left behind. The authors of ancient embroilments of the text were sad
bunglers indeed. In the meantime **ℵ** inadvertently also retained S.Luke's word
ΛΟΤΟΝ; and because **ℵ** here follows B in every other respect, **ℵ** exhibits a text
which is simply unintelligible.

Now the second clause of the sentence, viz, the words **οὐδε ἔχω τήν ψυχήν μου τιμίαν ἐμαυτῷ** may not on any account be surrendered, for it is indeed beyond the reach of suspicion, being found in Codd. A, D. E. h. L. P, 13, 31 — in fact in every known copy of the Acts except the discordant trio אBC. This clause is further witnessed to by the Vulgate, the Harkleian, by Basil, Chysostom, Cyril, Euthalius, and by the interpolator of Ignatius. What are we to think of our guides (Tischendorf, Tregelles, Westcott and Hort, etc.) who have in spite of these witnesses surrendered the Traditional Text and have instead presented us with what Dr. Field describes as the impossible reading, **ἀλλ οὐδενός λόγου ποιοῦμαι τήν ψυχήν τιμίαν ἐμαυτῷ**?

Dr. Field remarks, "modern Critics in deference to the authority of the older MSS., and to certain critical canons which prescribe that preference should be given to the shorter and more difficult reading over the longer and easier one, have decided that the T.R. in this passage is to be replaced by that which is contained in those older MSS. In regard to the difficulty of this reading, that term seems hardly applicable to the present case. A difficult reading is one which presents something apparently incongruous in the sense, or anomalous in the construction, which an ignorant or half-learned copyist would endeavor by the use of such critical faculty as he possessed to remove; but which a true critic is able, by probably explanation, and a comparison of similar cases, to defend against all such fancied improvements. In the reading before us it is the construction, and not the sense, which is in question; and this is not simply difficult — *it is impossible!* There is really no way of getting over it; it baffles novices and experts alike."

When will men believe that a reading vouched for by only BאC is safe to be a fabrication? But at least when Copies and Fathers combine, as here they do, against those three, what can justify critics in upholding a text which carries on its very face its own condemnation[1]?

Luke 2:14 The Angelic Hymn

We now come to the inattention of those long-since-forgotten first and second century scribes who, beguiled by the similarity of the letters **EN** and **AN** in the expression **EN ANθρωποις εὐδοκια** left out the preposition. An unintelligible clause was the consequence, which someone then sought to remedy by adding to **εὐδοκία** the sign of the genitive (C). Thus the Old Latin translations were made.

That this is the true history of a blunder which the latest editors of the New Testament have mistaken for genuine Gospel, is certain. Most Latin copies exhibit *pax hominibus bonae voluntatis*, as well as many Latin Fathers. On the other hand the preposition **EN** is retained in every known copy of S. Luke without exception, while the reading **εὐδοκία** is absolutely limited to the four uncials ABאD.

The witness of antiquity on this head is overwhelming and decisive:
In the second century the Syriac Versions and Irenaeus support the Received Text. In the third century, the Coptic Version, Origin in 3 places, and the Apostolical Constitutions in 2 places, do the same. In the fourth century (to which century B and א belong) Eusebius, Aphraates the Persian, Titus of Bostra, each in two places — Didymus in 3; Gregory of Nazianzus, Cyril of Jer, and Epiphanius in 2 places — Gregory of Nyssa 4 times; Ephraem Syr., Philo bp. of Carpasus, Chrysostom 9 times, and an unknown Antiochian contemporary of his — these eleven are every one in support of the Received Text. In the fifth century, besides the Armenian Version, Cyril of Alex. in 14 places;

Theodoret in 4; Theodotus of Ancyra in 5; Proclus; Paulus of Emesa; the Eastern bishops of Ephesus collectively, A.D. ; and Basil of Seleucia — these contemporaries of Cod. A are all eight in support of the Received Text. In the sixth century, besides the Georgian and Ethiopic Versions, Cosmas 5 times; Anatasius Sinait. and Eulogius, contemporaries of Cod. D are all in support of the Received Text. In the seventh and eighth centuries, Andreas of Crete; pope Martinus at the Latin Council; Cosmas of Mauiume near Gaza, and his pupil John Damascene; together with Germanus, abp. of Constantinople; are again all five in support of the Received Text.

To these 35 must be added 18 other ancient authorities of uncertain date, but *all* of considerable antiquity, and some are proved by internal evidence to belong to the fourth or fifth centuries — in short to be of the date of the Fathers whose names 16 of them severally bear, but among whose genuine works their productions are probably *not* to be reckoned. One of these was anciently mistaken for Gregory Thaumaturgus; a second for Methodius; a third for Basil. Three others with different degrees of reasonableness have been supposed to be Athanasius. One has passed for Gregory of Nyssa; another for Epiphanius; while no less than eight have been mistaken for Chrysostom, some of them being certainly his contemporaries. Add one anonymous Father, and the author of the apocryphal *Acta Pilati*, and it will be perceived that 18 ancient authorities have been added to the list, every whit as competent to witness what was the text of S. Luke 2:14 at the time when A, B,ℵ,D were written, as Basil or Athanasius, Epiphanius or Chrysostom themselves. For our present purpose they are as Codices of the fourth, fifth and sixth centuries. In this way, then, far more than 53 ancient witnesses have come back to testify to the men of this generation that the commonly received reading of S Luke 2:14 is *the true reading*, and that the text which the Critics are seeking to palm off on us is *a fabrication and a blunder*. Will any one be found to maintain that the authority of B and ℵ is appreciable when confronted by the first 15 ecclesiastical writers enumerated above? Or can A stand against the seven which follow.?

This is not all, however. Survey the preceding witnesses geographically. Note that one name is from Gaul; 2 from Constantinople; 5 are dotted over Asia Minor; ten at least represent Antioch, and six other parts of Syria; three are from Palestine, and 12 for other churches of the East; at least five are Alexandrian; two are from Cyprus and one is from Crete. If the articulate voices of so many illustrius bishops, coming back to us in this way from every part of ancient Christendom, and all delivering the same unfaltering message — if this is not allowed to be decisive on a point of the kind now before us, then pray let us have it explained to us. What amount of evidence *will* men accept as final? The truth is plain, that a case has been established against ℵ B A D and the Latin version which amounts to *proof* that those documents, even when they conspire to yield the self-same evidence, are not to be depended on as witnesses of the text of Scripture.

Mark 15:6; 6:22

In other cases the source, the very progress of the blunder, is discoverable. Thus whereas S. Mark in 15:6 certainly wrote ἕνα δέσμιον, ΟΝΠΕΡ ἡτοῦτο, the scribe of Δ, who evidently derived his text from an earlier copy in uncial letters is found to have divided the Evangelist's syllables wrongly, and to exhibit in this place ΟΝ ΠΕΡΗΤΟΥΝΤΟ. The consequence might have been predicted. ℵ B and A transform this into ΟΝ ΠΑΡΗΤΟΥΝΤΟ, which accordingly is the reading adopted by Tischendorf and Westcott and Hort.

Whenever, in fact, the final syllable of one word can possibly be mistaken for the first syllable of the next, or *vice versa*, it is safe to assume that sooner or later it has misled somebody. So we are not at all surpised to find S. Mark's **ὃ παρέλαβον** in Mark 7:4 transformed into **ἅπερ ἔλαβον**, but only in **B**.

Another startling instance of the same phenomenon is supplied by the substitution in S. Mark 6:22 of **τῆς θυγατρὸς αυτοῦ Ἡρωδιάδος** for **τῆς θυγατρὸς αὐτῆς τῆς Ἡρωδιάδος**. Here a first copyist left out **τῆς** as being a repetition of the last syllable of **αὐτῆς**, and afterwards a second copyist attempted to improve the Greek by putting the masculine pronoun for the feminine (**ΑΥΤΟΥ** for **ΑΥΤΗΣ**). The consequence was hardly to have been foreseen. For it strangely results in the following monstrous figment; that the fruit of Herod's incestuous connection with Herodias had been a daughter, who was also named Herodias; and that she as the king's own daughter was the immodest one who came in and danced before him and his lords as they sat at the birthday banquet. Probability, natural feeling, the obvious requirements of the narrative, and history itself — for Josephus expressly informs us that Salome, not Herodias was the name of the daughter — these all reclaim loudly against such a perversion of the truth. But the testimony of the MSS. settle the question, for only seven (אBDLΔ and two cursive copies) can be found to exhibit this strange mistake. Accordingly the reading **ΑΥΤΟΥ** is rejected by Griesbach, Lachmann, Tregelles, Tischendorf and Alford, but nevertheless found favor with Dr. Hort.

This is indeed another instructive instance of the effect of accidental errors, another proof that אBDL cannot be trusted.

This recurrence of identical or similar syllables near together was a frequent source of error. Copying has always a tendency to become mechanical. And when the copyist's mind sank to sleep in his monotonous toil, as well as if it became too active, the sacred Text suffered more or less, and so even a trifling mistake might be the seed of serious depravation.

Mark 8:1; 7:14; John 13:37

Another interesting and instructive instance of error originating in sheer accident is supplied by the reading in certain MSS. of S. Mark 8:1. That the Evangelist wrote **παμπόλλου ὄχλου** *("the multitude being very great")* is certain. This is the reading of all the uncials but eight, of all the cursives but fifteen. But instead of this it has been proposed that we read "when there was again a great multitude." It is plain that some ancient scribe mistook the less usual compound word for what was to himself a far more familiar expression; that is he mistook **ΠΑΜΠΟΛΛΟΥ** for **ΠΑΛΙΝ ΠΟΛΛΟΥ**. This blunder must date from the second century, for *iterum* is met with in the Old Latin as well as in the Vulgate, the Gothic, the Bohairic, and some other versions. On the other hand it is against "every true principle of Textual Criticism" (as Dr. Tregelles would say), that the more difficult expression should be abandoned for the easier, when forty-nine out of every fifty MSS. are observed to uphold it; when the oldest version of all, the Syriac, is on the same side; the source of the mistake is so patent; and when the rarer word is observed to be in S. Mark's peculiar manner. There could be in fact no hesitation on this subject if the opposition had not been headed by those notoriously false witnesses אBDL, which is now the fashion to uphold at all hazards. They happen in this instance to be supported by GMNΔ and fifteen cursives; while two other cursives look both ways and exhibit **πάλιν παμπόλλου.**

In S. Mark 7:14 **πάλιν** was similiarly misread by some copyists for **πάντα**, and has been preserved by ℵBDLΔ (ΠΑΛΙΝ for ΠΑΝΤΑ) against thirteen uncials, all the cursives, the Peshitto and Armenian versions. So again in S. John 13:37, A reads δύνασαί μοι by an evident slip of the pen for δύναμαί σοι. And in S. John 19:31 μεγαλΗ Η Ημερα has become μεγάλη ὑμέρα in ℵAEΓ and some cursive copies.

CHAPTER 2 FOOTNOTES

Page 14: ¹Surprising it is how largely the text of this place has suffered at the hands of Copyists and Translators. In A and D the words ποιοῦμαι and ἔχω have been made to change places. D introduces μοι after ἔχω; has ἐμαυτοῦ for εψθμαυτῷ; exhibits τοῦ τελειῶσαι without ὡς. C writes ὡς τό τελειῶσαι. ιB alone of the Codexes present us with τελειώσω for τελειῶσαι, and are followed by Westcott and Hort *alone of all Editors*. The Peshitto and the Ethiopic get rid of τιμίαμ as well as of οὐδὲ ἔχω. So much diversity of text, and in such primitive witnesses, while it points to a remote period as the date of the blunder, yet it testifies eloquently to the utter perplexity which that blunder occasioned from the first.

CHAPTER 3

ACCIDENTAL CAUSES OF CORRUPTION

HOMOEOTELEUTON (Likeness of Ending)

No one who finds the syllable **OI** recurring six times over in about as many words is surprised to learn that MSS. of a certain type exhibit serious perturbation in that place. Accordingly **BLΞ** leave out the words **καὶ οἱ ἄνθρωποι**; and in that mutilated form the modern critical editors are contented to exhibit S. Luke 2:15. One would have thought that Tischendorf's eyes would have been opened when he noticed that in his own Codex **ℵ** another **οι** is dropped, and by this nonsense is made of the passage (*viz.* **οἱ ἄγγελοι ποιμένες**). It is evident that a line with a *like ending* has been omitted by the copyist of some very early codex of S. Luke's Gospel, [skipping from **OI ΑΓΓΕΛΟI** to **ποιμενες** leaving out either **ΚΑΙ ΟΙ ΑΝΟΙ ΟΙ** or else **ΚΑΙ ΟΙ ΑΝΟΙ** and putting the other **OI** with **ΠΟΙΜΕΝΕ**.

Another such place is found in S. John 6:11. The Evangelist certainly described the act of our Saviour on a famous occasion in the well-known words

καὶ εὐχαριστήσας διέδωκε

τοῖς {μαθηταις,

οἱ δὲ μαθηται

τοῖς} ανακειμενοις

It is clear that some scribe has allowed his eye to wander from **τοῖς** in line 2 to **τοῖς** in line 4, and by this S. John is made to say that our Saviour Himself distributed to the 5,000. But the testimony of the MSS. proves the Received Text to be right, and moreover we are expressly assured by S. Matt. 14:19, S. Mark 6:41 and S. Luke 9:16 that dealt out the loaves to the disciples to distribute.

The blunder is a very ancient one, for it has crept into the Syriac, Bohairic and Gothic versions, besides many copies of the Old Latin; and has established itself in the Vulgate. And some Fathers (beginning with Origen) so quote the place. But **ℵBABLΠ** are contradicted by D and twelve other uncials, beside the body of the cursives, the Ethiopic and two copies of the Old Latin, as well as Cyril Alex.

There does not exist a source of error which has proved more fatal to the transcribers of MSS. than the proximity of identical, or nearly identical, combinations of letters. And because these are generally met with in the final syllables of words, the error referred to is familiarly known by a Greek name denoting 'likeness of ending' (Homoeoteleuton). The eye of a scribe on reverting from his copy to the original before him is apt sometimes to alight on the same word, or what looks like the same word, a little lower down. The consequence is obvious; all that should have come in between gets omitted, or sometimes it is duplicated. However inconvenient it may prove to find five, ten, twenty, perhaps thirty words omitted in this way, at times no serious consequence ensues. But the result is often sheer nonsense. When this is the case, it is usally admitted by all. A single example may stand for a hundred; In S John 6:55 that most careless of careless transcripts, Cod. **ℵ** omits seven words, and thus makes nonsense, causing the Scriptures to say "my flesh is drink indeed." The transcriber of **ℵ** let his eye pass from one **ἀληθῶς** to another, and characteristically enough the various correctors of this corrupt MS. allowed the error to remain until it was removed in the seventh century.

But occasions must inevitably occur when the result is calamitous, and even perplexing in the extreme. The writings of Apostles and Evangelists, and the Discourses of our Divine Lord Himself abound in short formulae. The intervening matter on such occasions is constantly an integral part of the message. Occasionally such may be discovered from the context without evident injury to the general meaning of the place. In this way verse 14 of S. Matt. chapter 23 was omitted in an early age, owing to the recurrence of οὐαὶ ὑμῖν at the beginning by some copyists. The error was repeated in the Old Latin versions. It passed to Egypt, as some of the Bohairic copies, the Sahidic and Origen testify. The Vulgate is quite consistent, and of course that concord of bad witnesses (especially in S. Matt.) ℵBDLZ follow suit, in company with the Armenian, the Lewis, and five or more cursives — enough to make the more emphatic the condemnation by the main body of the cursives. Besides the verdict of the cursives, thirteen uncials including Φ and Σ, the Peshitto, Harkleian, Ethiopic, Arabian, some MSS. of the Vulgate, with Origen (iii. 838, only in Lat.), Chrysostom (vii. 707 *bis*; ix. 755); Opus Imperf. 185 *bis*; 186 *bis*; John Damascene (ii. 517); Theophylact (i. 124); Hilary (89; 725); Jerome (iv. 276; v. 52; vi. 138; vii. 185).

Worst of all it will sometimes of necessity happen that such an omission took place at an exceedingly remote period, for there have been careless scribes in every age. And consequently the error is pretty sure to have propagated itself widely. If it is observed to be in several of the known copies — and if it is discoverable in two or more of the 'old uncials,' — all hope of its being easily extirpated is ended. Instead of being recognized as a blunder — which it clearly is — it is forthwith charged upon the Apostle or the Evangelist, as the case may be. In other words, it is taken for granted in some quarters that the clause in dispute can have had no place in the sacred autograph. It is from that time forward treated as an unauthorized accretion to the text. It is quite idle to appeal to the ninety-nine copies out of a hundred which contain the missing words.

Matthew 19:9 an Instance of Homoeoteleuton

In S. Matt. 19:9 our Saviour had declared that whoever puts away his wife, except for fornication, then added these words: καὶ ὁ ἀπολελυμένην γαμήσας μοιχᾶται ("*and shall marry another, commits adultery*"). Those five words are not found in Codd. ℵDLS, nor in several copies of the Old Latin, nor in some copies of the Bohairic and the Sahidic. Tischendorf and Tregelles accordingly reject them. Yet it is perfectly certain that the words are genuine. Those thirty-one letters probably formed three lines in the oldest copies of all. For they are observed to exist in the Syriac (Peshitto, Harkleian and Jerusalem), the Vulgate, some copies of the Old Latin, the Armenian and the Ethiopic versions, besides at least seventeen uncials, including ΒΦΣ, and the vast majority of the cursives. There can be no question of the genuineness of the clause.

Luke 16:21

A somewhat graver instance of omission resulting from the same cause is seen in S. Luke 16:21, where there is a threefold recurrence of the letters τῶν: ΤΩΝ ψιχίων ΤΩΝ πιπτόντΩΝ. This evidently resulted in the dropping of the words ψιχίων τῶν from some copies. Unhappily the sense is not destroyed by the omission. It is therefore not surprising to discover that the words are missing from ℵBL, or to find that they are supported here by copies of the Old Latin, and as usual by the Egyptian versions, nor by Clemens Alex and the author of the Dialogus. On the other hand Jerome condemns the Latin reading, and the Syriac Versions are observed to approve Jerome's verdict, as well as the Gothic. But what settles the question is the fact that every known Greek MS. except those three witnesses against the omission — as do Ambrose, Eusebius, Alex, Gregory Naz., Asterius, Basil, Ephraim Syr., Chrysostom, and Cyril of Alexandria. So it is perplexing to discover, and distressing to have to record, that all the recent Editors of the Gospels are more or less agreed in abolishing *"the crumbs which fell from the rich man's table."*

The foregoing instances are but to afford specimens of the influence of *accidental causes* on the transmission from age to age of the Text of the Gospels. Before the sense of the exact expressions of the Written Word was impressed on the collective mind of the Church — when the Canon was not definitely defined and acknowledged, and the halo of antiquity had not yet gathered around writings which had been recently composed — severe accuracy was not to be expected. Errors would be sure to arise, especially from accident, and early ancestors of these errors would be certain to have a numerous offspring. Besides the evil would increase, and slight deviations would give rise in the course of natural development to serious and perplexing corruptions.

CHAPTER 4

ACCIDENTAL CAUSES OF CORRUPTION:
FROM WRITING IN UNCIAL CHARACTERS

Corrupt readings have occasionally resulted from the ancient practice of writing Scripture in the uncial character, without accents, without punctuation, and indeed without any division of the text or spacing between words. These corruptions are especially found in places where there is something unusual in the structure of the sentence.

John 4:35, 36

John 4:35, 36 has suffered in this way, due to the position of ἤδη. Certain of the scribes who imagined that this word might belong to verse 36 rejected the καί at the beginning of verse 36 as being superfluous; though no Father is known to have been guilty of such a solecism. Others, aware that ἤδη can only belong to verse 35, were not unwilling to part with the copula at the beginning of verse 36. A few, considering both words of doubtful authority, retained neither[1]. In this way it has come to pass that there are four ways of exhibiting this place:

πρὸς θερισμὸν ἤδη. Καὶ ὁ θερίζων
πρὸς θερισμὸν ἤδη ὁ θ.
πρὸς θερισμὸν ἤδη. Ὁ θερίζων
πρὸς θερισμόν. Ὁ θερίζων, κ.τ.λ.

The only point of importance however is the position of ἤδη. This is claimed for verse 35 by the great mass of the copies, as well as by Origen, Eusebius, Chrysostom, Cyril, the Vulgate, Jerome, and the Syriac. The Italic copies are hopelessly divided here, and Codd. אBmΠ do not help us. But ἤδη is claimed for verse 36 by CDEL, 33, and by the Curetonian and Lewis; while Cod. A is singular in beginning verse 36 with both words, ἤδη καί, which shows that some early copyist, with the correct text before him, adopted a vicious punctuation. For there can be no manner of doubt that the commonly received text and the usual punctuation is the true one. On careful review every unprejudiced reader will allow this. But recent critics are for leaving out καί, with אBCDL; while Tischendorf, Westcott/Hort and Tregelles are for putting the full stop after πρὸς θερισμόν, and with ACDL making ἤδη begin the next sentence. But as Alford finds out, this is clearly inadmissible.

Sometimes this affects the translation. So the Revisers propose in the parable of the prodigal son; "And I perish *here* with hunger." But why *here?* it is because the earliest copies of Luke was written: ΕΓΩΔΕΛΙΜΩΑΠΟΛΛΥΜΑΙ. But some careless scribe after writing ΕΓΩΔΕ then reduplicated the last three letters, ΩΔΕ, mistaking them for an independent word. Accordingly in the Codex Beza, in R and U, and about ten cursives, we encounter εγω δε ωδε. The inventive faculty having thus done its work, it remained to superadd the transposition we see in אBL —from εγω δε ωδε λιμω, the sentence then was developed into εγω δε λιμω ωδε. And this is approved by Griesbach, Schultz, Lachmann, Tischendorf, Tregelles, Alford and Westcott and Hort in succession. it is a very ancient blunder, for it is found in the Latin and the Syriac translations; therefore it must date from the second century. But nevertheless it is a blunder, a blunder which 16 uncials and the whole body of the cursives bear emphatic witness. Having detected its origin, we now trace its progress;

The inventors of ὧδε or other scribes quickly saw that this word requires a correlative in the earlier part of the sentence. So the same primitive 'authorities' which advocate *here* are observed also to advocate above *"in my father's house."* no extant Greek copy is known to contain those words ἐν τῷ οἴκῳ, but such copies must have existed in the second century. The Peshitto, and Cureton and Lewis recognize these three words, as well as copies of the Latin which Jerome, Augustine and Cassian were acquainted with. The phrase *in domo patris mei* has accordingly established itself in the Vulgate. But surely we of the Church of England who have until now been spared this second blunder may reasonably refuse to take the first downward step. Our Lord did not intend any contrast whatever between two localities, but between two parties. The comfortable estate of the hired servants were being set against the abject misery of the son; not the house in which the servants dwelt with the spot where the poor prodigal was standing. But if hesitation to accept the foregoing verdict lingers in any quarter, it ought to be dispelled by a glance at the context in ℵBL. What else but the instinct of a trained understanding is it to survey the neighborhood of a place like the present? in verse 16 we discover that ℵBDLR present us with χορτασθηναι εκ for γεμίσαι τὴν κοιλίαν αθτοῦ ἀπό. Then in verse 22 is made to say to his father by ℵBDUX Ποίησόν με ὡς ἕνα τῶν μισθίων σου. The prodigal was prepared to say this, but his father's kindness stopped him, therefore he did not say what ℵBDUX makes him say. In addition ℵBLX and the Old Latin are for thrusting in ταχυ after ἐξενέγκατε. Are not these one and all confessedly fabricated readings? Are they not the infelicitous attempts of some well-meaning critic to improve on the inspired original?

John 5:44

From the fact that three words in S. John 5:44 were in the oldest MSS. written; **MONOYΘYOY** (that is, μόνου Θεοῦ οὐ, the middle word, θεοῦ, got omitted from some very early copies. By this the sentence is made to say in English "And seek not the honor which comes from the only One." It is so that Origen, Eusebius and Didymus, besides the two best copies of the Old Latin, exhibit the place. As to Greek MSS. the error survives only in B at the present, thus preserving an old Alexandrian error.

Acts 27:14

In Acts 27:14 S. Luke explains that it was a typhonic wind called Euroclydon which caused the ship in which S. Paul and he sailed past Crete to incur the harm and loss so graphically described there. That wind is mentioned nowhere but in this one place. Its name, however, is sufficiently intelligible, being compounded of Εὖρος, the south-east wind, and κλύδων, a tempest. This compound happily survives intact in the Peshitto version. The Syriac translator, not knowing what the word meant, copied what he saw, "the blast of the tempest," which blast is called Tophonikos Euroklidon. But the licentious scribes of the West did not do so, but insisted on extracting out of the actual Euroclydon the imaginary name of Euro-quillo, and so it stands to this day in the Vulgate. But Jerome did not so read the name of the wind, or he would hardly have explained *Eurielion* or *Euriclion* to mean *commiscens, sive deorsum ducens*. Codexes ℵ and A are at this day the sole surviving witnesses to the perversion of **ΕΥΡΟΚΛΥΔΩΝ** into **ΕΥΡΑΚΥΛΩΝ**. It is well that the fabricated word is scanty, for Euro-aquillo collapses the instant it is examined. nautical men point out that it is "inconsistent in its construction with the principles on which the names of the intermediate or compound winds are framed" — *"Euronotus* is so called as intervening immediately between *Eurus* and *Notus*, and as partaking, as was thought, of the qualities of both. The same holds true of *libonotus* as being interposed between *Libs* and *Notus*. Both these compound winds lie in the same quarter or quadrant of the circle with the winds of which they are composed, and no other wind intervenes. But *Eurus* and *Aquilo* are at 90 degrees distance from one another, or according to some writers at 105 degrees; for *Eurus* lies in the southeast quarter, and *Aquilo* in the northeast; also two winds, one of which is the East cardinal point, intervene, as Caecias and Subsolanus [2]. Further, why should the wind be designated by an impossible *Latin* name in a Greek setting. The ship was out of Alexandria; the sailors were Greek. Then what business did *Aquilo* have here? Next, if the wind did bear the name of Euroaquilo, why is it introduced in this marked way as if it were a kind of curiosity? Such a name would utterly miss the point, which is the violence of the wind as expressed in the term Euroclydon. But if S.Luke wrote **EYPAK-** how has it come to pass that every copyist but three has written **EYPOK-**? The testimony of **B** is memorable: the original scribe wrote **EYPAKYΔΩN**: the second corrected this into **EYPYKΛYΔΩN**, which is also the reading of Euthalius. The essential circumstance is that *not* **YΛΩN** but **YΔΩN** has all along been the last half of the word in Codex **B** [3].

In S. John 4:15, on the authority of ₁**B** Tischendorf adopts **διέρχεσθαι** instead of **ἔρχεσθαι**, assigning as his reason that no one would ever have substituted the compounded verb for the uncompounded one. But to construct the text of Scripture on such considerations is to build a lighthouse on a quicksand. I could have referred the learned Critic to plenty of places where the thing he speaks of as incredible has been done. The proof that S. John used **ἔρχεσθαι** is the fact that it is found in all the copies except ₁**B**, those untrustworthy MSS. The explanation of the corrupt **Διερχωμαι** can be accounted for by the final syllable of the preceding word (**μηδέ**).

Similar corruptions have occurred in these places also:

S. Mark 10:16 **ευλογει** has become **κατευλογει** (in ₁**BC**)
S. Mark 12:17 **θαυμασαν** has become **εξεθαυμασαν** (in ₁**B**)
S. Mark 14:40 **βεβαρημενοι** has become **καταβεβαρημενοι** (A₁**B**)

It is impossible to doubt that **και** is indebted to its existence to the same cause in modern critical editions of Luke 17:37. In the phrase **ἐκεῖ συναχθήσονται οἱ ἀετοῖ** it might have been predicted that the last syllable of **ἐκεῖ** would some day be mistaken for the conjunction **και**. And so it has actually come to pass, as **ΚΑΙ οι αετοι** is met with in many ancient authorities. But ℵ**BL** also transpose the clauses and also substituted **επισυναχθηθησονται** for **συναχθήσονται**. The self-same casualty, that is **και** being elicited out of **εκει**, and the transposition of clauses, is seen among the cursives at S. Matt. 24:28, the parallel place — where the old uncials distinguish themselves by yet graver eccentricities (such as, **οπου—ου** ₁; **γαρ** (**γαρ** ₁**BDL**); **εαν—(αν—D**); **το πτωρα** (**σωμα-** ℵ). How can we as judicious critics ever think of disturbing the text of Scripture on evidence so precarious as this?

Matthew 22:23

It is proposed that we should henceforth read S. Matt. 22:23 as follows; "on that day there came to him Sadducees *saying* that there is no Resurrection." A new incident would be in this way introduced into the Gospel narrative, resulting from a novel reading of the passage. instead of **οἱ λέγοντες**, we are invited to read **λέγοντες**, on the authority of **אBDMSZP** and several of the cursives, besides Origen, Methodius, Eiphanius. This is a respectable array. Nevertheless, there is a vast preponderance of numbers in favor of the usual reading, which is also found in the Old Latin and the Vulgate. But surely the discovery that in the parallel Gospels it is: **οἵτινες λέγουσιν ἀνάστασιν μὴ εἶναι** (S. Mark 12:18) and in S. Luke 20:27, **οἱ ἀντιλέγοντες ἀνάτασιν μὴ εἶναι**, thus making it decisive that the T.R. reading is correct. I am sure it will be so regarded by anyone who has paid close attention to the method of the Evangelists. Add that the origin of the mistake is seen the instant the words are inspected as they must have stood in an uncial copy: **ΣΑΔΔΟΥΚΑΙΟΙΟΙΛΕΓΟΝΤΕΣ** —then really nothing more needs be said, because it is safe to say the second **ΟΙ** got dropped in a collocation of letters like that. It might also have been anticipated that there would be found copyists who would be confused by the antecedent **ΚΑΙ**. Accordingly the Peshitto, Lewis and Curetonian render the place *'et dicentes;'* showing that they mistook **ΚΑΙ ΟΙ ΛΕΓΟΝΤΕΣ** for a separate phrase.

CONFUSION CAUSED BY VERBS ENDING IN ΤΟ

The termination **ΤΟ** in certain tenses of the verb, when followed by the neuter article, naturally leads to confusion; sometimes to uncertainty. In S. John 5:4 for instance, where we read in our copies **καὶ ἐτάρασσε τό ὕδωρ**, but so many MSS. read **ἐταράσσετο**, that it becomes a perplexing question as to which to follow. The sense in either case is excellent, the only difference being whether the Evangelist actually says that the Angel *"troubled"* the water, or leaves it to be inferred from the circumstance that after the Angel had descended, instantly the water *"was troubled."*

The question becomes less difficult of decision when (as in S. Luke 7:21) we have to decide between two expressions; **ἐχαρίσατο βλέπειν** (which is the reading of **א*ABDEG** and 11 other uncials) and **ἐχαρίσατο το βλέπειν** (which is only supported by **א** by the second corrector, and ELVA). The bulk of the cursives faithfully maintain the former reading, and merge the article in the verb.

Luke 23:11; 23:27; Matthew 4:23

In the expression **ἐσθῆτα λαμπρὰν ἀνέπεμψεν** (Luke 23:11), we are not surprised to find the first syllable of the verb (**αν**) absorbed by the last syllable of the immediately preceding **λαμπράν**. Accordingly **אLR** supported by one copy of the Old Latin and a single cursive concur in displaying **ἔπεμψεν** in this place.

The letters **ΝΑΙΚΩΝΑΙΚΑΙ** in the expressing **γυναικῶν αἴ καὶ** (Luke 23:27) could be expected to produce confusion. The first of these three words could of course take care of itself (though D, with some of the versions, make it into **γυναικες**). Not so with what follows, for ABCDLX and the Old Latin (except c) drop the **και**. **א**and C drop the **αι**. The truth rests with the fourteen remaining uncials and with the cursives.

So also the reading **εν ολη τη Γαλιλαια** (B) in S. Matt. 4:23 is due simply to the reduplication on the part of some inattentive scribe of the last two letters of the immediately preceding word (**περιηγεν**). yet Lachmann, Tischendorf, Tregelles, Alford, Westcott/Hort, etc. adopt the reading of **B**. The received reading of the place is correct; **καὶ περιῆγεν ὅλην τὴν Γαλιλαίαν ὁ Ἰησοῦς** — because the first five words are so exhibited in all the copies except

B℘C; and those three differ, as usual, from one another (and this alone should be deemed fatal to their evidence):

B reads: καὶ περιῆγεν ἐν ὅλῃ τῇ Γαλιλαία

℘ reads; καὶ περιῆγεν ὁ ἰς ἐν τῇ Γαλιλαία

C reads: καὶ περιῆγεν ὁ ἰς ὅλῃ τῇ Γαλιλαίᾳ

But what about the position of the Sacred Name; how is it that ὁ 'Ιησοῦς, which comes after Γαλιλαίαν in almost every known copy, should instead come after περιῆγεν in three of these MSS. (D₁C) and in the Latin, Peshitto, Lewis and Harkleian? Since B leaves out Jesus altogether, we find Tischendorf, Alford, Westcott/Hort and the Revisers doing the same. But a thoughtful inquirer is sure to ask why is the order disturbed in ₁CD. It is because in the twin place in S.Matt. (9:35) we find καὶ περιῆγεν ὁ ἰς familiar. So familiar had this order of the words become that the scribe of ₁ has even introduced the expression into S. Mark 6:6, the parallel place, where ὁ clearly has no business. I give these minute details because it is the only way to make the subject before us understood. This is another instance where the 'Old Uncials' show that their text is corrupt. Again we must resort to the cursives to find accuracy in transcription.

2 Peter 1:21

The introduction of ἀπό instead of ἅγιοι in 2 Peter 1:21 derives its origin from the same prolific source. For some ancient scribe mistook the first four letters of αγιοι for απο (ΑΓΙΟ for ΑΠΟ). After 1,700 years the only copies witnessing to this deformity are BP with four cursives. In opposition are ℘AKL and the whole body of the cursives, the Vulgate, and the Harkleian. Euthalius did not know of it. It is obvious that next some perplexed one introduced both readings (απο and αγιοι). So we find απο θεου αγιοι in C, two cursives, and Didymus. Then another variant crops up, putting υπο for απο — but only because υπο went immediately before. Theophylact is the sole patron of this blunder. The consequence of all this might have been foreseen: from just a few codexes, both απο and αγιοι were left out, and this accounts for the reading of certain copies of the Old Latin. Tischendorf and his followers seem unaware of how the blunder began, so they claim that the last three variants prove the authenticity of the first. Therefore, they would have us read "men spoke *from* God" instead of the true reading, *"holy men of God spoke."* Is it not clear that any reading attested by only B and P and four cursives must be self-condemned? Another excellent specimen of this class of error is furnished by Heb. 7:1. Instead of 'Ο συναντήσας 'Αβραάμ, ℘BAD exhibit ΟΣ. The whole body of the copies, headed by CLP are against them, besides Chrysostom, Theodoret, Damascene. This reading arose because the initial letter of συναντήσας has been reduplicated through careless transcription (ΟΣΣΥΝ instead of ΟΣΥΝ). That is all. But it is instructive to note that it is the four oldest of the uncials that propagated this palpable blunder.

Matthew 27:7

This last specimen is second to none in suggestiveness. Pilate asked, "Whom will you that I release to you?" But in an early age we discover that some copies of the Gospel proceeded this way: "Jesus [who is called] Barabbas, or Jesus who is called Christ?" Origen so quotes the place, then proceeds to write "In many copies mention is not made that Barabbas was also called Jesus, and those copies may perhaps be right — else would the name of

Jesus belong to one of the wicked — of which no instance occurs in any part of
the Bible. Nor is it fitting that the name of Jesus should like Judas have been
borne by saint and sinner alike." Then Origen adds, "I think something of this
sort must have been an interpolation of the heretics." From this we are clearly
intended to infer that "Jesus Barabbas" was the prevailing reading of S. Matt.
27:7 in the time of Origen, a circumstance which we pronounce incredible,
apart from the fact that a multitude of copies existed besides those used by
Origen[4].

The sum of the matter is probably this: Some inattentive second century
copist [probably a Western translator into Syriac who was an indifferent
Greek scholar] mistook the final syllable of "unto you" (**YMIN**) for the word
Jesus (displayed in uncials as **IN**). In other words he carelessly reduplicated
the last two letters of **YMIN**. Origen caught sight of the extravagance and
condemned it, though he fancied it to be prevalent. And the thing slept for
1,500 years until just fifty years ago Drs. Lachmann, Tischendorf and
Tregelles construct that 'fabric of Textual Criticism' which has been the cause
of this present treatise. But as everyone must see such things as these are not
'readings' at all, nor even the work of 'the heretics,' but are simply
transcriptional mistakes. How Dr. Hort, admitting the blunder, yet pleads that
'this remarkable reading is attractive by the new and interesting fact which it
seems to attest, and by the antithetic force which it seems to add to the question
in verse 17" is more than we can understand. To us the expression seems most
repulsive. No 'antithetic force' can outweigh our dislike to the idea that
Barabbas the murderer was our Saviour's namesake!

CHAPTER 4 FOOTNOTES

Page 21: [1]It is clearly unsafe to draw any inference from the mere omission of ἤδη in ver. 35, by
those Fathers who do not show how they would have begun ver. 36 (as Eusebius, Theodoret and
Hilary.

Page 23: [2]Falconer's Dissertation on S. Paul's Voyage, pp. 16 and 12.

Page 23: [3]True, that the compounds *eurenotus eyroauster* exist in Latin. That is the reason why the
Latin translator (not understanding the word) rendered it *Euroaquilo*, in stead of writing *Euraquilo*.
I have no doubt that it was some Latin copyist who began the mischief, like the man who wrote ἐπ᾽
αὐτῷ φόρῳ for ἐπ᾽ αὐυτοφώρῳ.

Page 26: [4]The only evidence, so far as I can find, for reading *Jesus* Barrabas (in S. Matt. 27:16, 17)
are five disreputable Evangelia 1, 118, 209, 241, 299 — the Armenian Version, the Jerusalem
Syriac, and the Sinai Syriac.

CHAPTER 5

ACCIDENTAL CAUSES OF CORRUPTION OF THE TEXT: ITACISM

The art of transcription on vellum did not reach perfection until after the lapse of many centuries in the life of the Church. Even in the minute elements of writing much uncertainty prevailed during a great number of successive ages. It by no means follows that, if a scribe possessed a correct auricular knowledge of the Text, he would therefore exhibit it correctly on parchment. Copies were largely disfigured with misspelled words. And vowels especially were interchanged. Accordingly, such change became in many instances the cause of corruption, and this is known in Textual Criticism as ITACISM.

The casual reader may think that undue attention is being paid to minute particulars. But it constantly happens that from such exceedingly minute and seemingly trivial mistakes serious misrepresentations of the Holy Spirit's meaning have occurred. This may include new incidents introduced into the Scriptures. unheard-of statements, name changes, and other perversions of our Lord's Divine sayings — such phenomena are observed to follow upon the mere omission of the article, or the insertion of an expletive, or the change of a single letter. For instance, παλιν, when thrust in where it has no business, makes it appear that our Saviour promised to return the ass on which He rode in triumph into Jerusalem (Mark 11:4). When our Lord was about to enter into His capital in lowly triumph, He gave to two of His disciples directions well calculated to suggest the mysterious nature of the incident which was to follow. They were to go to a certain village, to unloose a certain colt, and to bring the creature immediately to Jesus. If encountered they were to simply announce that *"the Lord has need of him."* But, singular to relate, this transaction is found to have struck some third-rate third-century Critic as not altogether correct. He was evidently of the opinion that the colt ought in common fairness to have been returned to the owners of it as soon as the purpose had been accomplished for which it had been obtained. Availing himself of the fact that there was no nominative before "will send" in S. Mark 11:3, this Critic assumed that it was *of Himself* that our Lord was still speaking, and so he feigned that the sentence is to be explained this way: "say . . .that the Lord has need of him and will immediately send him hither." So in this view our Savior instructed His two disciples to convey to the owner of the colt that *He would send the creature back as soon as He had finished with it*; that is, the colt would be *but a loan*. But by way of clenching the matter the Critic proceeded on his own responsibility to thrust into the Scripture text the word *again* (παλιν) The fate of such an unauthorized accretion might have been predicted. After skipping about in quest of a fixed resting-place for a few centuries (אDL and C* and B and Δ all have different variations, but all keep παλιν in their texts. But it was effectually eliminated from the copies. Traces of it linger on in those MSS. cited above, and about a dozen cursive copies (also of a depraved type). But the fabrication is so transparent it ought to have been long since forgotten. Yet our modern-day revisionists have not been afraid to revive it. Of what can they have been dreaming? They cannot pretend that they have *Antiquity* on their side, for besides all the copies, with A at their head, both the Syriac versions, both the Latin versions, and both the Egyptian versions, the Gothic, the Armenian are against them. Even Origen, who twice himself inserts πάλιν, also twice leaves it out.

By writing ω for ο many critics have transferred some words from the lips of Christ to those of His Evangelist, and thus made Him say what He never would have dreamed of saying (καθαρίζων for καθάριζον, 7:19 of S. Mark's Gospel.

By subjoining ς to a word in a place which it has no right to fill, the harmony of the heavenly choir has been marred effectually, and a sentence produced which defies translation (Luke 2:14, previously discussed).

By omitting τῷ and Κύριε, the repenting malefactor is made to say, "Jesus! Remember me when Thou comest in Thy kingdom" (Luke 23:42)

Speaking of our Saviour's triumphal entry into Jerusalem, which took place the day after S. John says that Lazarus sat at the table with Him, and there *"the multitude which had been with Him when He called Lazarus out of the tomb and raised Him from the dead bore testimony"* (S. John 12:1,2,17). The meaning of this is explained by Luke 19:37, 38, where it is said that the sight of so many acts of Divine power moved the crowds to give memorable testimony, especially because of the raising of Lazarus from the dead. But Tischendorf and Lachmann, who on the authority of D and four later uncials read ὅτι instead of ὅτε, import into the Gospel quite another meaning. According to their way of exhibiting the text, S. John is made to say: "the multitude which was with Jesus testified *that* He called Lazarus out of the tomb and raised him from the dead" — which is not only an entirely different statement, but also introduces a highly improbable circumstance. It is not denied that many copies of the Old Latin (but not the Vulgate) recognize ὅτι, besides the Peshitto and the two Egyptian versions. This is in fact only one more proof of the insufficiency of such collective testimony. אAB with the rest of the uncials, and what is of more importance, the whole body of the cursives, exhibit ὅτε (when) — and that is certainly what S. John wrote in this place. Tischendorf's assertion that the prolixity of the expression is inconsistent with ὅτε may surprise, but it will never convince anyone who is even moderately acquainted with S. John's peculiar manner.

The same mistake of ὅτι for ὅτε is met with at S. John 12:41: *'These things said Isaiah because* he saw His glory." And why not *when* he saw His glory? This last is what the Evangelist wrote, according to the strongest attestation. It is true that eleven MSS, beginning with אBAL, and the Egyptian versions exhibit ὅτι; also Nonnus. But all other MSS., the Latin, Peshitto, Gothic, Ethiopic, Georgian, and one Egyptian version — also Origen, Eusebius in four places, Basil, Gregory of Nyssa twice, Didymus three times, Chrysostom twice, Severianus of Gabala. These twelve versions and Fathers constitute a body of ancient evidence which is overwhelming. Cyril three times reads ὅτι, three times ὅτε, and once ἡνίκα, which proves at least how he understood it.

[Unfortunately, though the Dean left several lists of instances of Itacism, he worked out none, except the substitution of ἕ for ἐν in Mark 4:8. And as it is not strictly on all fours with the rest, I have reserved it until last. he mentioned all that I have introduced (besides a few others), some of them more than once. In the brief discussion of each instance which I have supplied, I have endeavoured whenever it was practicable to include any slight expressions of the Dean's that I could find, and to develop all surviving hints — Edward Miller, original editor]

A suggestive example of the corruption introduced by a petty Itacism may be found in Rev. 1:5, where the beautiful expression which has found its way into so many tender passages relating to Christian devotion, *"Who has washed us from our sins in His own blood "* has been replaced in many critical editions by "Who has *loosed* us from our sins by His blood." In early times a purist scribe, who had a dislike of anything that savored of provincial retention of Aeolian or Dorian pronunciations, wrote from unconscious bias **u** for **ou**, thereby transcribing **λύσαντι** instead of the correct **λούαντι** (unless he were not Greek scholar enough to understand the difference). And he was followed by others, especially those who, whether from their own prejudices or due to sympathy with the scruples of other people, but in any case under the influence of a slavish literalism, hesitated about a passage in which they did not rise to the precious meaning really conveyed in it. So we find the three uncials which are nearest the period of corruption adopt it, and they are followed by nine cursives, the Harkleian Syriac, and the Armenian versions. On the other side are two uncials, B/2 of the eighth century and P of the ninth, and the Vulgate, Bohairic, Ethiopic versions — and what is most important — all the other cursives.

Luke 15:24, 32; 16:25; John 13:25

An instance where an error from an Itacism has crept into the Received Text may be seen in S. Luke 16:25. Some scribes needlessly changed **ὧδε** into **ὅδε**, misinterpreting the letter which served often for both the long and the short **o**, and thereby cast out some illustrative meaning, since Abraham meant to lay stress on the enjoyment of comfort in his bosom by Lazarus. The unanimity of the uncials, a majority of the cursives, the witness of the versions, are sufficient to prove that **ὧδε** is the genuine word.

Again, in S. John 13:25, **οὕτως** has dropped out of many copies and so out of the Received Text because by an Itacism it was written **οὕτος** in many manuscripts. So **ἐκεῖνος οὗτος** was thought to be a clear mistake, and the weaker word was accordingly omitted. No doubt Latins and others who did not understand Greek well considered also that **οὕτως** was redundant, and this was the cause of its being omitted in the Vulgate. But really **οὕτως**, being sufficiently authenticated by **BCEFGHLMXΔ** and most cursives, is exactly in consonance with the Greek usage and S. John's style, and adds considerably to the graphic character of the sacred narrative. S. John was reclining on his left arm over the bosom of the robe of the Saviour. When S. Peter beckoned to him, he turned his head for the moment and sank (**ἐπιπεσών**, not **ἀ ναπεσών** which has the testimony only of **B** and about twenty-five uncials, **ℵ** and C being divided against themselves) on the breast of the Lord, being still in the general posture in which he was (**οὗτος**), and asked Him in a whisper, *"Lord, who is it?"*

Mark 4:8

Another minute but interesting indication of the accuracy and fidelity with which the cursive copies were made is supplied by the constancy with which they witness to the preposition **ἐν** (*not the numeral, ἕν*) in S. Mark 4:8. Our Lord says that the seed which *"fell into the good ground yielded by* (**ἐν**) thirty, and by (**ἐν**) sixty, and by (**ἐν**) an hundred." Tischendorf notes that besides all the uncials which are furnished with accents and breathings (viz. EFGHKMUVΠ) "nearly 100 cursives" exhibit **ἐν** here and in verse 20. But this is to misrepresent the case. All the cursives may be declared to exhibit **ἐν**, e.g. all Matthaei's and all Scrivener's. I have personally, with this object in mind, examined a large number of Evangelia, and I found **ἐν** in all of them. The Basle MS. from which Erasmus derived his text exhibits ἐv, though he printed ἔv out of respect for the Vulgate. The Complutensian having ἔv, the reading of the Received Text follows in consequence. But the traditional reading has been shown to be ἐv, which is no doubt intended by EN in Cod. A. Codd. אCΔ (ever licentious, and Δ particularly throughout S. Mark) substitute for the preposition ἐv the preposition εἰς (a sufficient proof to me that they understand EN to represent ἐv, not ἔn). And these are followed by Tischendorf, Tregelles, and the Revisers. As for the libertine B and its servile henchman L, for the first ἐv (but not for the second and third) it substitutes εἰς; while in verse 20 it retains the first ἐv, but omits the other two. In all these vagaries B is followed by Westcott and Hort[1].

Titus 2:5

In his epistle to Titus S.Paul directs that young women shall be *"keepers at home"* (οἰκουρούς). So every known Codex, except five, including the corrected א and D, HKLP; besides 17, 37, 47. So also Clemens Alex., Theodore of Mopsuestia, Basil, Chrysostom, Theodoret, Damascene. So again the Old Latin, the Vulgate, and Jerome; and so the Peshitto, and the Harkleian versions and the Bohairic. There evidently can be no doubt whatever about a reading supported like this. To be οἰκουρός was held to be a woman's chiefest praise. On the contrary gadding about from house to house is what the Apostle expressly condemns (1 Tim. 5:13). But of course the decisive consideration is not the support derived from internal evidence, but the plain fact that antiquity, variety, respectability, numbers, continuity of attestation, are all in favor of the traditional reading.

Notwithstanding this overwhelming evidence Lachmann, Tischendorf, Tregelles and Westcott/Hort are for thrusting that barbarous and scarcely intelligible word, οἰκουργούς into Titus 2:5. The Revised Version in consequence exhibits "workers at home," which Dr. Field may well call an "unnecessary and most tasteless innovation." But it is insufficiently attested as well, besides being a plain perversion of the Apostle's teaching.

Matthew 8:29

In the cry of the demoniacs (S. Matt. 8:29), the name Jesus is omitted by Bא. The reason is plain the instant an ancient MS. is inspected, in uncial letters it would be: ΚΑΙΣΟΙΙΥΥΙΕΤΟΥΘΥ, in which the recurrence of the same letters evidently caused too great a strain to scribes, and the omission of two of them was the result of ordinary human infirmity.

Indeed to this same source are to be attributed an extraordinary number of so-called 'various readings;' but which in reality are nothing but a collection of mistakes. They are the surviving tokens that anciently copying clerks left out words — whether misled by the proximity of a like ending, or by the speedy recurrence of the like letters, or by some other phenomenon with which most men's acquaintance with books have long since made them familiar.

CHAPTER 5 FOOTNOTES

[1] [The following specimens taken from the first hand of B may illustrate the kakigraphy, if I may use the expression, which is characteristic of that MS. and also of א. The list might be easily increased.

I. *Proper Names.*

Ιωανης, generally: Ιωαννης, Luke i. 13*, 60, 63; Acts iii. 4; iv. 6, 13, 19; xii. 25; xiii. 5, 25; xv. 37; Rev. i. 1, 4, 9; xxii. 8.

Βεεζεβουλ, Matt. x. 25; xii. 24, 27: Mark iii. 22; Luke xi. 15, 18, 19.

Ναζαρετ, Matt. ii. 23; Luke i. 26; John i. 46, 47. Ναζαρα, Matt. iv. 13.

Ναζαρεθ, Matt. xxi. 11; Luke ii. 51; iv. 16.

Μαρια for Μαριαμ, Matt. i. 20; Luke ii. 19. Μαριαμ for Μαρια, Matt. xxvii. 61; Mark xx. 40; Luke x. 42; xi. 32; John xi. 2; xii. 3; xx. 16, 18. See Traditional Text, p. 86.

Κουμ, Mark v. 41. Γολγοθ, Luke xix. 17.

Ιστραηλειται, Ιστραηλιται, Ισραηλειται, Ισραηλιται.

Ελεισαβετ, Ελισαβετ.

Μωσης, Μωυσης.

Δαλμανουνθα, Mark viii. 10.

Ιωση (Joseph of Arimathea), Mark xv. 45. Ιωσηφ, Matt. xxvii. 57, 59; Mark xv. 42; Luke xxiii. 50; John xix. 38.

II. *Mis-spelling of ordinary words.*

καθ' ιδιαν, Matt. xvii. 1, 19; xxiv. 3; Mark iv. 34; vi. 31, &c. κατ' ιδιαν, Matt. xiv. 13, 23; Mark vi. 32; vii. 33, &c.

γενημα, Matt. xxvi. 29; Mark xiv. 25; Luke xxii. 18. γεννημα, Matt. iii. 7; xii. 34; xxiii. 33; Luke iii. 7 (the well-known γεννήματα εχιδνων).

A similar confusion between γένεσις and γέννησις, Matt. i, and between εγενήθην and εγεννήθην, and γεγένημαι and γεγέννημαι. See Kuenen and Cobet N. T. ad fid. Cod. Vaticani lxxvii.

III. *Itacisms.*

κρείνω, John xii. 48 (κρεινεῖ). κρίνω, Matt. vii. 1; xix. 28; Luke vi. 37; vii. 43; xii. 57, &c.

τειμῶ, τιμῶ, Matt. xv. 4, 5, 8; xix. 19; xxvii. 9; Mark vii. 6, 10, &c.

ενεβρειμήθη (Matt. ix. 30) for ενεβριμήσατο. ανακλειθῆναι (Mark vi. 39) for ανακλῖναι. σεῖτος for σῖτος (Mark iv. 28).

IV. *Bad Grammar.*

τῷ οἰκοδεσπότῃ επεκάλεσαν for τὸν οἰκοδεσπότην εκάλ. (Matt. x. 25). καταπατήσουσιν for -σωσιν (Matt. vii. 6). ὃ ἂν αἰτήσεται (Matt. xiv. 7). ὅταν δὲ ἀκούετε (Mark xiii. 7).

V. *Impossible words.*

εμνηστευμένην (Luke i. 27). ουρανοῦ for ουρανίου (ii. 13). ανηζήτουν (Luke ii. 44). κοπιοῦσιν (Matt. vi. 28). ηρώτουν (Matt. xv. 23). κατασκηνοῖν (Mark iv. 32). ημεῖς for υμεῖς. υμεῖς for ημεῖς.]

CHAPTER 6
ACCIDENTAL CAUSES OF CORRUPTION:
LITURGICAL INFLUENCE

There is one distinct class of evidence provided by Almighty God for the conservation of the deposit in its integrity, which calls for special notice in this place. The lectionaries of the ancient Church have not yet nearly enjoyed the attention they deserve, or the laborious study they absolutely require to render them practically available. Scarcely any persons except professed critics are at all acquainted with the contents of these very curious documents. And the collations of any of them have been until now effected by few indeed. I speak chiefly of the Books called Evangelistaria, or Evangeliaria; in other words, the proper lessons collected out of the Gospels, and transcribed into a separate volume. let me freely admit that I subjoin a few observations on this subject with unfeigned diffidence, having had to teach myself the little I know of them. And in the end I have discovered how very insufficient for my purpose my knowledge of these is. Properly handled, an adequate study of the Lectionaries of the ancient Church would become the labor of a life. We require exact collations of at least 100 of them. From such a practical acquaintance with about a tenth of the extant copies some very interesting results would infallibly be obtained.

As for the external appearance of these documents, it may be enough to say that they range, like the mass of uncial and cursive copies, over a space of about 700 years — the oldest being of about the eighth century, and the latest dating in the fifteenth. Rarely are any so old as the eighth, or so recent as the fifteenth. It is not known when they began to be executed, but older copies than those now existing must have perished through constant use. They are almost invariably written in double columns, and not unfrequently are splendidly executed. The use of uncial letters is observed to have been retained in documents of this class to a later period than in the case of the Evangelia, that is, down to the eleventh century. For the most part they are furnished with a kind of musical notation executed in vermilion, which is evidently intended to guide the reader in that peculiar recitative which is still customary in the oriental church.

In these books the Gospels always stand in the following order: John; Matthew; Luke; Mark. The lessons are brief, resembling the Epistles and Gospels in our Book of Common Prayer.

They seem to fall into two classes: (a) those which contain a lesson for every day in the year; (b) those which only contain lessons for fixed festivals and the Saturday-Sunday lessons. We are reminded by this peculiarity that it was not until a very late period in her history that the Eastern Church was able to shake herself clear of the shadow of the old Jewish Sabbath. To these Lectionaries Tables of the Lessons were often added. The Table of the daily Lessons went under the title of Synaxarion; and the Table of the Lessons of the Immovable Festivals and Saints' days was styled Monologion. Contents of these Tables may be seen in Scrivener's Plain Introduction, 4th ed., pp. 80-89. The textual student will remember that besides the Lectionaries of the Gospels, of which about 1,000 are known, there are some 300 more of the Acts and Epistles, called by the name of Apostolos.

Liturgical use has proved a fruitful source of textual perturbation. Nothing less was to have been expected, as everyone must admit who has examined ancient Evangelia. For the period before the custom arose of writing out the Ecclesiastical Lessons in the Evangelistaries and Apostolos, it may be regarded as certain that it was the general practice to accommodate an ordinary copy of the Gospels, or of the Epistles, to the requirements of the Church. This continued to the last to be a favorite method with the ancients. Not only was it the invariable liturgical practice to introduce an ecclesiastical lection with an ever-varying formula, but notes of time, and of some passages regarded as carrying no moral lesson, were omitted. And at times the holy Name is found in MSS. where it has no proper place.

That Lessons from the New Testament were probably read in the assemblies of the faithful according to a definite scheme, and on an established system, at least as early as the fourth century, has been shown to follow from plain historical fact.

Cyril at Jerusalem, and his namesake at Alexandria, Chrysostom, Augustine — all these expressly witness to this early practice. in other words there is found to have been at least at that time these Lectionaries throughout the churches of Christendom. And they seem to be essentially one and the same in the West and the East. That it may have been of even Apostolic antiquity may be inferred. For example, Marcion the heretic, in A.D. 140, would hardly have constructed an Evangelistarium and Apostolicon of his own, as we learn from Epiphanius (i.311,) if he had not been induced by the Lectionary system prevailing around him to form a counterplan of teaching on the same model.

EXAMPLES OF LITURGICAL INFLUENCE ON THE TEXT

Indeed, the high antiquity of the Church's Lectionary System is inferred with certainty from many a textual phenomenon known by students of textual science. It may be helpful if I introduce the class of readings to be discussed in the present chapter, by inviting attention to the first words of the Gospel of St. Philip and St. James' Day in our English Book of Common Prayer: "And Jesus said to His disciples." Those words are undeniably nothing else but an Ecclesiastical accretion to the Gospel. And yet they have stood prefixed to S. John 14:1 from an exceedingly remote period. For besides establishing themselves in every Lectionary of the ancient Church, they are found in Cod. D/2, in copies of the Old Latin, and in copies of the Vulgate. They may be of the second or third centuries, but they must certainly be as old as the fourth century. It is evident that but for a very little those words could have been given a permanent place in the Text. Readings just as slenderly supported have actually been adopted by some[1]. Another instance: and here the success of an ordinary case of Lectionary licence will be perceived to have been complete. For besides recommending itself to Lachmann, Tischendorf, Tregelles and Westcott/Hort, this blunder has established itself in the pages of the Revised Version. I refer to an alteration of the Text occurring in certain copies of Acts 3:1. This gross depravation of the Text resulted from liturgical influence, and was occasioned by the adding of words at the beginning of the chapter. The Peshitto, the most ancient witness accessible, confirms the usual reading of the place, which is also the text of the cursives: Ἐπὶ τὸ αὐτὸ δὲ Πέτρος καὶ Ἰωάννης, etc. So the Harkleian and Bede, and Cod. E. But four of the oldest uncials conspire in representing the words which immediately precede in the following unintelligible fashion: ὁ δὲ Κύριος προσετίθει

τοὺς σωζομένοθς καθ ἡμέραν ἐπί τό αὐτό. Πέτρος δέ κ.τ.λ.
How could such a strange and vapid presentment of this passage have had its beginning? I answer, from the ecclesiastical practice of beginning a fresh lection at the name of Peter, with the prefatory words, "In those days." It is accordingly usual to find the liturgical word ἀρχή to indicate the beginning of a lection, and in this case it is thrust in between ἐπί τό αὐτό δέ and Πέτρος. I suppose that at some earlier period a more effectual severance of the text was made in that place, and that this unhappily misled some early scribe. And so it came to pass that in the first instance the place stood this way: ὁ δὲ Κύριος προσετίθει τοὺς σωζομένους καθ' ἡμέραις ταύταις Πέτρος κ.τ.λ.. The scribe in that place with simplicity both gave us the liturgical formula usually introducing the Gospel for the Friday after Easter, and permitting us to witness the perplexity with which the evident surplus words (τῇ ἐκκλησίᾳ τό αὐτό)occasioned him. So he inverts those two expressions and thrusts in a preposition. How obvious it now was to solve the difficulty by getting rid of "the church."

It does not help the adverse case to show that the Vulgate as well as Cyril of Alexandria's copy are disfigured with the same corrupt reading as אBAC. It only proves how early and how widespread is this depravation of the Text. But the indirect proof obtained from the actual Lectionaries shows the corruption dates far before our oldest Codexes. I suspect that it was in Western Christendom that this corruption of the text had its beginning, for proof is not lacking that the expression ἐπί τό αὐτό seemed hard to the Latins.

LITURGICAL INFLUENCE ON THE ENDING OF MARK

By far the most considerable injury which has resulted to the Gospel from Lectionary use is the suspicion which has alighted in certain quarters on the last twelve verses of S. Mark. For those verses made up a complete Lection by themselves. The preceding Lection, which was used on the Second Sunday after Easter, was closed with the Liturgical note: "The End" (ΤΟ ΤΕΛΟΣ), and this occurred after the eighth verse. What is more probable; yea more certain, than that some scribe should mistake the end of the Lection for the end of S. Mark's Gospel, especially if the last leaf of the Lection had been torn off, or separated. How natural that S. Mark should express himself in a more condensed and abrupt style than usual. This is put forth only as an explanation, one which leaves the notion of another writer and a later date unnecessary.

Luke 7:31

In the whole compass of the Gospel there is not any more interesting instance than what is furnished by the words εἶπε δὲ ὁ κύριος in Luke 7:31. This is certainly derived from the Lectionaries. For it is nothing else than the word formula with which it was customary to introduce the lection that begins at this place. Only one out of forty copies that I have examined contain these words, yet they are found in the Received Text. But interesting it is to note that when these four *unauthorized* words have been gotten rid of, then it is revealed that the two preceding verses (28 and 29)form a part of our Lord's continuous discourse from verse 24 through verse 35. Wordsworth has noted this, but Alford and Westcott/Hort doubt it. But the fact does not admit of rational doubt. We learn from the 24th verse that our Saviour was at this time addressing "the crowds" (multitudes). But the four classes specified in verses 29 and 30 cannot reasonably be thought to be S. Mark's analysis of those crowds. What is said of the Pharisees and Lawyers in verse 30 is clearly a remark made by our Saviour about the reception given to John the Baptist by the common people and the publicans on the one hand, and of the Pharisees and Scribes on the other. So we see the inferential particle οὖν in the 31st verse, and in verse 35 the same verb, ἐδικαιώθη, which the Lord had employed in verse 29. And by this He takes up His previous statement while He applies and enforces it.

Another specimen of unauthorized accretion originating in the same way is found a little further on. In S. Luke 9:1 we read, "And having called together His twelve Disciples, etc." But the words "disciples of Him" (μαθητὰς αὐτοῦ) are confessedly spurious, for they are condemned by nearly every known cursive and uncial. Their presence may be fully accounted for by the rubrical direction as to how the lesson is to be introduced, which reads: "At that time Jesus having called together His twelve Disciples" (a note that appears adjacent to the place in the Text). Accordingly we are not surprised to find the words ὁ 'Ιησοῦς *also* thrust into a few of the MSS. But we are hardly prepared to discover that the words of the Peshitto, besides the Latin and the Cureton's Syriac, are disfigured in the same way. The admirers of the old uncials will learn with interest that instead of "His disciples," ℵC with LXΛΞ and a choice assortment of cursives exhibit "apostles" — and are supported in this manifestly spurious reading by the best copies of the Old Latin, the Vulgate, Gothic, Harkleian, Bohairic, and a few other translations.

LITURGICAL INFLUENCE ON SOME CORRUPTIONS OF COD. ℵ

It is surprising what a fertile source of corruption Liturgical usage has proved. Careful students of the Gospels will remember that S. Matthew describes our Lord's first and second missionary journeys in very nearly the same words. S. Matt. 4;23 ends with καὶ πᾶσαν μαλακίαν ἐν τῷ λαῷ, and is used to conclude the lesson for the second Sunday after Pentecost. S. Matt. 9:35 ends with καὶ πᾶσαν μαλακίαν, and occupies the same position in the Gospel for the seventh Sunday. It will not seem strange to anyone considering the matter that ἐν τῷ λαῷ has not only found its way into S. Matt. 9:35, but has established itself there very firmly, and that from a very early time. These spurious words are first met with in the Codex ℵ.

But sometimes corruptions of this class are really perplexing. Thus ℵ testifies to the existence of a short additional clause (καὶ πολλοὶ ἠκολούθησαν αὐτῷ) at the end of S. Matt. 9:35, as some critics claim. But are we not rather to regard these words as the beginning of verse 36, and as being nothing else but the liturgical introduction to the lection for the Twelve Apostles, which follows (9:36-10:8)? Whatever its origin, this confessedly spurious accretion to the Text, which exists only in L and six cursive coies, it must be of extraordinary antiquity because it is found in the two oldest copies of the Old Latin. This, again, is an indication that the antiquity of a spurious addition is insufficient to prove it is a genuine representation of the true Text.

This is the reason why such a strange amount of discrepancy is discoverable in the first words of S. Luke 10:35 (καὶ ἰδοὺ νομικός τις ἀνέστη, ἐκπειράζων αὐτόν, καὶ λέγων) in certain of the oldest documents. many of the Latin copies preface this with *et haec eo dicente*. Now the established formula of the lectionaries here is: νομικός τις προσῆλθεν τῷ, which explains why the Curetonian, the Lewis, with 33, their usual leader in aberrant readings, so read the place; while D, with one copy of the Old Latin, alone exhibits ἀνέστη δέ τις νομικός. Four codexes (ℵBLΞ) with the Curetonian omit the second καί. To read this place in its purity you have to take up any ordinary cursive copy.

Mark 15:28

Mark 15:28 has been read in all churches as follows: "*And the Scripture was fulfilled, which says, . . . And He was numbered with the transgressors.*" In these last days, however, the discovery is announced that every word of this is an 'unauthorized addition' to the inspired text. Griesbach indeed only marks the verse as probably spurious; Tregelles is content to enclose it in brackets. But Alford, Tischendorf, Westcott/Hort and the Revisers eject the words from the text altogether. What can be the reason for so extraordinary a proceeding?

Let us not be told by Schulz (Griesbach's latest editor) that 'the quotation is not in Mark's manner; that the formula which introduces it is John's; and that it seems to be a gloss taken from Luke 22:37.' This is not criticism! It is dictation — imagination, not argument. Men who so write forget that they are assuming the very point which they are called upon to prove.

Now it happens that all the uncials but six, and an immense majority of the cursive copies contain the words before us. Besides these, the Old Latin, the Syriac, the Vulgate, the Gothic and Bohairic versions all concur in exhibiting them. These words are expressly recognized by the Sectional System of Eusebius, having a section to themselves — and this is the weightiest sanction that Eusebius had it in his power to give to words of Scripture. They are also recognized by the Syriac sectional system, which is diverse and independent from that of Eusebius. What then is to be set against such a weight of ancient evidence? The fact that the following six Codexes are without this 28th verse: אBACDX, together with the Sahidic and the Lewis. The notorious Codex k (Bobiensis) is the only other ancient testimony producible, to which Tischendorf adds 'about forty-five cursive copies.' Will it be seriously pretended that this evidence for omitting verse 28 from S. Mark's Gospel can compete with the evidence for retaining it? Say not again that we set numbers against antiquity. Codex D is of the sixth century; X not older than the ninth; and not one of the four remaining Codexes cited against the verse are as old as the Old Latin or the Peshitto versions (not perhaps within two centuries as old). We have Eusebius and Jerome's Vulgate as witnesses on the same side, besides the Gothic version (which represents a Codex probably as old as either). To these witnesses must be added Victor of Antioch, who commented on S. Mark's Gospel before either A or C were written.

It will be not unreasonably asked by those who have learned to regard whatever is found in B and א as oracular: 'But is it credible that on a point like this such authorities as אBACD should all be in error?' It is not only credible, but a circumstance of which we meet with often, finding so many undeniable examples that it ceases even to be a matter of surprise. On the other hand, what is to be thought of the creditibility that on a point like this all the ancient versions, except the Sahidic, should have conspired to mislead mankind? And on what intelligible principle is the consent of all the other uncials, and the whole mass of the cursives, to be explained, if this verse of Scripture is indeed spurious?

I foresee the rejoinder. They will say, 'Yes, but if the ten words in dispute really are part of the inspired verity, how is their absence from the earliest Codexes to be accounted for? It happens for once I am able to assign the reason. But I do so under protest, for I insist that to point out the source of the mistakes in our oldest Codexes is no part of a critic's business. It would only prove an endless, and also a hopeless task.

EXPLANATION: If the reader will take the trouble to inquire at the Bibliotheque at Paris for a Greek Codex numbers '71,' an Evangelium will be put into his hands which differs from any that I ever met with in giving singularly minute and full rubrical directions. At the end of S. Mark 15:27, this is written: 'When you read the sixth Gospel of the Passion — also when you read the second Gospel of the Vigil of Good Friday — stop here; skip verse 28, then go on at verse 29.' The inference from this is so obvious that it would abuse the reader's patience to enlarge on it, or even to draw it out in detail. Very ancient indeed must have been the Lectionary practice in this particular; so much so that it would leave so fatal a trace in its operation in our four oldest Codexes. But *it has left it!*ⁿ The explanation is evident; the verse is plainly genuine. And the Codexes that leave it out are corrupt.

One word about the evidence of the cursive copies on this occasion. Tischendorf says that 'about forty-five' of them are without this precious verse of Scripture. I venture to say that the learned critic would be puzzled to produce forty-five copies of the Gospels in which this verse has no place. But in fact his very next statement (that 'about half of these are Lectionaries,) satisfactorily explains the matter. For these words are away from every Lectionary in the world, as well as in every MS. which, like B and ℵ has been depraved by the influence of Lectionary practice.

And now I venture to ask: What is to be thought of our Revisers who omit verse 28 altogether; with a marginal intimation that 'many ancient authorities insert it'? Would it not have been the course of ordinary reverence — of truth and fairness — to leave the text unmolested, with a marginal memorandum saying that just 'a very few ancient authorities leave it out'?

Acts 3: 1

A gross depravation of the Text resulting from Lectionary practice has imposed on several critics, and this is illustrated by the first words of Acts 3. The most ancient witness accessible, namely the Peshitto version, confirms the usual reading of the place, which is also the text of the cursives: "*And on the same Peter and John,*" etc. So the Harkleian and Bede and Codex E. But the four oldest of the six available uncials conspire in representing the words which immediately precede in the following unintelligible fashion: **ὁ δὲ Κύριος προσετίθει τοὺς σωζομένους καθ' ἡμέραν ἐπὶ τὸ αὐτό. Πέτρος δὲ κ.τ.λ.** How is it to be thought that this strange and vapid presentment of the passage had its beginning? It results from the ecclesiastical practice of beginning a fresh lection at the name of Peter, prefaced by the usual Lectionary formula, 'In those days.' It is accordingly usual to find the liturgical word **ἀρχή** — indicative of the beginning of a lection — thrust in between **ἐπὶ τὸ αὐτό δὲ** and **Πέτρος**. At a yet earlier period I suppose some more effectual severance of the text was made in that place, and this unhappily misled some early scribe. And so it came to pass that in the first instance the place stood this way: **ὁ δὲ Κύριος προσετίθει τοὺς σωζομένους καθ' τῇ ἐκκλησίᾳ ἐπὶ τὸ αὐτό** — which was plainly intolerable.

What I am saying will commend itself to any unprejudiced reader when it has been stated that Cod. D in this place actually reads as follows; **καθημέραν ἐπὶ τὸ αὐτὸ ἐν τῇ ἐκκλησίᾳ. Ἐν δὲ ταῖς ἡμέραις ταύταις Πέτρος κ.τ.λ.** — the scribe with simplicity here gives us both the liturgical formula with which it was usual to introduce the Gospel for the Friday after Easter, and also permitting us to witnesss the perplexity with which the evident surplus material occasioned him. So he inverts those two expressions and thrusts in a preposition. How obvious it now was to solve the difficulty by also getting rid of **τῇ ἐκκλησίᾳ**!

It does not help the adverse case to show that the Vulgate, as well as Cyril of Alexandria's copy, are disfigured with the same corrupt reading as אBAC. It only proves how early and how widespread is this depravation of the Text. But the indirect proof is afforded by the fact that the actual Lectionary System must date from a period long before our oldest Codexes were written, and this is far more important. I suspect that it was in Western Christendom that this corruption of the Text had its beginning. For proof is not lacking that the expression ἐπὶ τὸ αὐτό seemed hard to the Latins[2].

Matthew 13:43

The same cause may be assigned to the omission of παλιν from אBD in S. Matt. 13:43. A glance at the place in an actual Codex will explain the matter to a novice better than a whole page of writing:[3] ακουετω.. τελος παλιν. αρχη. ειπεν ο Κυριος την παραβολην ταυτην. Ομοια εστιν κ.τ.λ. The word παλιν, because it stands between the end (τελος) of the lesson for the sixth Thursday and the beginning (αρχη) of the first Friday after Pentecost, got left out [though everyone acquainted with Gospel MSS. knows that αρχη and τελος were often inserted in the text]. The second of these two lessons begins with ομοια [because παλιν at the beginning of a lesson is not wanted]. Here then is a singular token of the antiquity of the Lectionary System in the Churches of the Easter, as well as a proof of the untrustworthy character of Codd. אBD. The discovery that they are supported this time by copies of the Old Latin, Vulgate, Curetonian, Bohairic, Ethiopic, does but further show that such an amount of evidence in and by itself is wholly insufficient to determine the text of Scripture. Therefore, when Tischendorf in the preceding verse on the sole authority of אB and a few Latin copies, omitting the world ακουειν — and again in the present verse on very similar authority (viz. אD, Old Latin, Vulgate, Peshitto, Curetonian, Lewis, Bohairic, together with five cursives of aberrant character) transposing the order of the words παντα οσα εχει τωλει — I can but reflect on the utter insecure basis on which the Revisers and the school which they follow would remodel the inspired Text.

It is precisely in this way and for the selfsame reason that the clause καὶ ἐλυπήθησαν σφόδρα comes to be omitted from S. Matt. 17:23 in K and several other copies. The previous lesson ends at ἐγερθήσεται, and the next lesson begins at προσῆλθον.

CORRUPTION OF THE LORD'S PRAYER EXPLAINED

Matthew 6:13

The Ancient Liturgy of the Church has frequently exercised a corrupting influence on the text of Scripture. Here we will discuss the genuineness of the doxology with which the Lord's Prayer concludes in S. Matt. 6:13: ὅτι σοῦ ἐστιν ἡ Βασιλεία καὶ ἡ δύναμις καὶ ἡ δόζα εἰς τοὺς αἰῶνας. ἀμήν

These words have been rejected by critical writers as spurious for the past 360 years, in spite of the fact that S. Paul recognizes them in 2 Tim. 4:18 — which alone, one would have thought, should have been sufficient to preserve them from molestation.

The essential note of primitive antiquity at all events these fifteen words enjoy in perfection, being met with in all the copies of the Peshitto (second century) — and this is a far weightier consideration than the fact that they are absent from most of the Latin copies. Even of these however four (k f g q) recognize the doxology. It is also found in Cureton's Syriac and the Sahidic version; the Gothic, Ethiopic, Armenian, Georgian, Slavonic, Harkleian, Palestinian, Erpenius' Arabic, and the Persion of Tawos versions. It is also testified to in the Didache (with variations); Apostolical Constitutions (iii. 18-vii 25 with variations); in St. Ambrose and Caesarius. Chrysostom comments on the words without suspicion, and often quotes them; as does Isidore of Pelusium. See also Opus Imperfectum, Theophylact on this place, and Euthymius Zigabenus. And yet their true claim to be accepted as inspired is of course based on the consideration that they are found in ninety-nine out of a hundred of the Greek copies, including Π and Σ of the end of the fifth and the beginning of the sixth centuries. What then is the nature of the adverse evidence with which they have to contend, and which is supposed to be fatal to their claims?

Four uncial MSS. (אBDZ), supported by five cursives of bad character (1, 17, which gives Amen, 118, 130, 209), and all the Latin copies except four, omit these words. Thus it is being assumed that these 15 words must have found their way surreptitiously into the text of all the other copies in existence. But let me ask: Is it at all likely, or rather is it any way credible, that in a matter like this, all the MSS. in the world but nine should have become corrupted? No hypothesis is needed to account for one more instance of omission in copies which have been shown to exhibit a mutilated text on every page. But how will men pretend to explain an interpolation as universal as the present one? For these words can be traced as far back as the second century; they have been established without appreciable variety of reading in all the MSS; they have therefore found their way from the earliest time into every part of Christendom; they are met with in all the Lectionaries, and in all the Greek Liturgies. And they have so effectually won the confidence of the churches that to this hour it forms part of the public and private devotions of the faithful all over the world.

One and the same reply has been given to this inquiry ever since the days of Erasmus. A note in the Complutensian Polyglott (1514) expresses it with sufficient accuracy. There we read: "In the Greek copies, after *And deliver us from evi!* follows *For thine is the kingdom, and the power, and the glory, forever.* But it is to be noted that in the Greek liturgy, after the choir has said *And deliver us from evil*, it is the Priest who responds as above; and those words, according to the Greeks, the priest alone may pronounce. This makes it probable that the words in question are no integral part of the Lord's Prayer; but that certain copyists inserted them in error, supposing, from their use in the liturgy, that they formed part of the text."

In other words the critic's use of this note contends that men's ears have grown so fatally familiar with this formula from its habitual use in the liturgy, that they assumed it to be part and parcel of the Lord's Prayer. So this same statement has been repeated *ad nauseam* by ten generations of critics for 360 years. The words with which our Saviour closed His pattern prayer are accordingly rejected by these as an interpolation resulting from the liturgical practice of the primitive church. And this slipshod account of the matter is being universally acquiesced in by learned and unlearned readers alike at the present day.

From an examination of above fifty ancient oriental liturgies, it is found then that though the utmost variety prevails among them, yet that *not one* of them exhibits the evangelical formula as it stands in S. Matt. 6:13; while in some instances the divergences of expression are even extraordinary. Subjoined is what may perhaps be regarded as the typical eucharistic formula, derived from the liturgy which passes as Chrysostom's. Precisely the same form recurs in the office which is called after the name of Basil; and it is essentially reproduced by Gregory of Nyssa, Cyril of Jerusalem, and pseudo-Caesarius; while something very like it is found to have been in use in more of the churches of the East:

"*For thine is the kingdom, and the power and the glory,* Father, Son and Holy Ghost, now and always and *for ever* and ever. *Amen*."

But as everyone sees at a glance, such a formula as the foregoing, with its ever-varying terminology of praise — its constant reference to the blessed Trinity — its habitual **νυν και αει** — and its invariable **εις τους αιωνας των αιωνων** (which must be of very high antiquity, for it is mentioned by Irenaeus, and may be as old as 2 Tim. 4:18 itself;) the doxology which formed part of the church's liturgy, though transcribed 10,000 times, could *never* by possibility have resulted in the *un*varying doxology found in MSS. of S. Matt. 6:13: *For thine is the kingdom, and the power, and the glory, for ever. Amen.*

On the other hand, the inference from a careful survey of so many eastern liturgies is inevitable. The universal prevalence of a doxology of some sort at the end of the Lord's Prayer; the general prefix, *for thine*; the prevailing mention therein of *the kingdom, and the power, and the glory*; the inevitable reference to Eternity — all of this constitutes a weighty corroboration of the genuineness of the form in S. Matthew. Eked out with a confession of faith in the Trinity, and otherwise amplified as piety or zeal for doctrinal purity suggested, every liturgical formula of the kind is clearly seen to be derived from the form of the words in S. Matt. 6:13. But in no conceivable way could that briefer formula have resulted from the practice of the ancient Church. The thing is impossible!

What need is there to point out that the Church's peculiar method of reciting the Lord's Prayer in the public liturgy does supply the obvious and sufficient explanation of all the adverse phenomena of the case? It was the invariable practice from the earliest time for the choir to break off at the words, *But deliver us from evil.* The choir never pronounced the doxology. For that reason the doxology must have been omitted by the critical owner of the archetypal copy of S. Matthew from which nine extant Evangelia, Origen, and the Old Latin version originally derived their text. This is the sum of the matter. There can be no simpler solution of the alleged difficulty. That Tertullian, Cyprian, Ambrose recognize no more of the Lord's Prayer than they found in their Latin copies cannot create surprise. The wonder would be if they did.

Much stress has been laid on the silence of certain of the Greek Fathers concerning the doxology, although they wrote expressly on the Lord's Prayer; such as Origen, Gregory of Nyssa (but his words are doubtful—see Scrivener, *Introduction*, ii. p. 325, note 1); Cyril of Jerusalem and Maximus. Those who have attended to such subjects will however bear me most ready witness that it is never safe to draw inferences of the kind proposed from the silence of the ancients. What if they regarded a doxology, wherever found, as hardly a fitting subject for exegetical comment? But however their silence is to be explained, it is at least quite certain that the reason of it is not because their copies of S. Matthew were without the doxology. Does anyone seriously imagine that in A.D. 650, when Maximus wrote, Evangelia were in a different state from what they are at present?

The sum of what has been offered may be briefly stated: The perturbation of the text in S. Matt. 6:13 is indeed due to a liturgical cause. But then it is found that not the great bulk of the Evangelia, but only Codd. ℵBDZ, 1, 17, 118, 130, 209, have been victims of the corrupting influence. As usual it is the few, not the many copies, which have been led astray. Let the doxology at the end of the Lord's Prayer be therefore allowed to retain its place in the text without further molestation. Let no profane hands be any more laid on these fifteen precious words of the Lord Jesus Christ.

There yet remains something to be said on the same subject fior the edification of studious readers:

The history of the rejection of these words is in a high degree instructive. It dates from 1514, when the Complutensian editors, while admitting that the words were found in their Greek copies, banished them from the text *solely* in deference to the Latin version. In a marginal annotation they started the *hypothesis* that the doxology is a liturgical interpolation. But how is it possible, since the doxology is commented on by Chrysostom? They are saying, 'We presume that this corruption of the original text must date from an antecedent period.' The same adverse sentence, supported by the same *hypothesis* was reaffirmed by Erasmus, and on the same grounds, *but in his edition of the N.T. he allowed the doxology to stand*. As the years have rolled by, and Codexes DBZℵ have successively come to light, critics have waxed bolder and bolder in giving their verdict. First Grotius, Hammond, Walton; then Mill and Grabe; next Bengel, Wetstein, Griesbach; lastly Scholz, Lachmann, Tischendorf, Tregelles, Alford, Westcott and Hort, and the Revisers have denounced the precious words as spurious.

But how does it appear that tract of time has strengthened the case against the doxology? Since 1514 scholars have become acquainted with the Peshitto version of the second century; and by its emphatic verdict it disposes of the evidence borne by all but three of the Old Latin copies. The Didache of the first or second century; the Sahidic version of the third century; and the Apostolic Constitutions (2), follow on the same side. In the fourth century come Chrysostom, Ambrose, ps.-Caesarius, the Gothic version. After that Isidore, the Ethiopic, Cureton's Syriac; the Harkleian, Armenian, Georgian, and other versions, with Chrysostom (2), the Opus Imperfectum, Theophylact, and Eythymius (2) bring up the rear. Does anyone really suppose that two Codexes of the fourth century (Bℵ), which are notorious for their many omissions and general inaccuracy, are any adquate set-off against such an amount of ancient evidence? L and 33, generally the firm allies of BD and the Vulgate, forsake them at S. Matt. 6:13; and these dispose effectually of the adverse testimony of D and Z, which are also balanced by Φ and Σ. But at this juncture the case for rejecting the doxology breaks down; and when it is discovered that every other uncial and every other cursive in existence may be appealed to in its support, and that the story of its liturgical origin proves to be a myth — what must be the verdict of an impartial mind on a survey of the entire evidence?

The whole matter may be conveniently restated this way: Liturgical use has indeed been the cause of a depravation of the text at S. Matt. 6:13; but it proves on inquiry to be the very few MSS. — not the very many — which have been depraved.

Nor is anyone at liberty to appeal to a yet earlier period than is attainable by existing liturgical evidence, and to suggest that then the doxology used by the priest may have been the same with that which is found in the ordinary text of S. Matthew's Gospel. This may have been the case, or it may not. Meanwhile, the hypothesis, which fell to the ground when the statement on which it rested was disproved, is not now to be built up again on a mere conjecture. But if the fact could be ascertained, and I am not concerned to deny that such a thing is possible, it would only be a confirmation of the genuineness of the doxology. For why should the liturgical employment of the last fifteen words of the Lord's Prayer by the earliest churches be thought to cast discredit on their genuineness? In the meantime, the undoubted fact that for an indefinitely remote period the Lord's Prayer was not publicly recited by the people further than *But deliver us from evil* — a doxology of some sort being invariably added, but pronounced by the priest alone — this clearly ascertained fact is fully sufficient to account for a phenomenon so ordinary [found indeed so commonly throughout S. Matthew, to say nothing of occurrences in the other Gospels] as really not to require particular explanation, viz. the omission of the last half of S. Matt. 6:13 from Codexes אBDZ.

Luke 11:2-4

An instructive specimen of depravation of the text can be traced to the heretic Marcion's mutilated recension of S. Luke's Gospel. We entreat the reader's sustained attention to the license with which the Lord's Prayer as given in S. Luke 11:2-4 is exhibited by Codices אBACD. For every reason one would have expected that so precious a formula would have been found enshrined in the 'old uncials' in peculiar safety. Yet the copyists of those codices have not done so with peculiar reverence:

(a) D introduces the Lord's Prayer by interpolating the following paraphrase of S. Matt. 6:7: *"Use not vain repetitions as the rest; for some suppose that they shall be heard by their much speaking. But when you pray"* — after which portentous exordium.

(b) Bא omit the five words, *"Our," "which art in heaven,"*

(c) D omits the article τό before *name*; and supplements the first petition with the words 'upon us' — it also transposes the words *Thy kingdom*.

(d) B in turn omits the third petition, *'Thy will be done, as in heaven, also on the earth;"* which eleven words are retained by א, but it adds *so* before *also* and omits the article τῆς — in this finding for once an ally in ACD.

(e) א D write δός for δίδου (from Matthew).

(f) א omits the article τό before *day by day*.

(g) D, instead of *day by day* writes *this day* (from Matthew); and substitutes *debts* for *sins* (also from Matt.); and in place of *for [we] ourselves* writes *as also we* (again from Matthew).

(h) א shows its sympathy with D by accepting two-thirds of this last blunder, exhibiting *as also [we] ourselves*.

(i) D consistently reads *our debtors* in place of *everyone that is indebted to us*.

(j) B and א omit the last petition, *but deliver us from evil* — here they are unsupported by A C or D.

We decline to take account of lesser discrepancies. So then these five codices described as 'first-class authorities' are found to throw themselves into *six different combinations* in their departures from S. Luke's way of exhibiting the Lord's Prayer. Among them they contrive to falsify in respect of no less than 45 words, and yet *they are never able to agree among themselves as to any single various reading*. And *only once* are more than two of them observed to stand together in their variations — and this in the unauthorized omission of the article. They bear *solitary evidence* (unsupported by the others) in the case of 32 out of the 45 words. What need is there to declare that in every case of solitary evidence they give false witness? But the infatuation of the Critics cause them to take for gospel the vagaries of Codex **B**. Besides omitting the 11 words which **B** omits jointly with **א** Westcott and Hort erase from the Book of Life those other 11 precious words which are omitted by **B** only. And in this way they pass on the mutilations which the scalpel of Marcion the heretic used to reduce the Lord's Prayer some 1730 years ago (for the mischief can all be traced back to Marcion). Now this is being palmed off on the Church by the Revisionists as if it were the work of the Holy Ghost.

CHAPTER 6 FOOTNOTES

Page 37: ¹It is surprising to find so great an expert as Griesbach in the last year of his life so entirely misunderstanding this subject. See his Comment. Crit. Part ii. p. 190.

Page 38: ²Bede,Retr. 111.D (add. of ἐν τ. ἐκκλ.). Brit. Museum Addit. 16, 184.fol. 152*b* Vulgate.

Page 38: ³So the place stands in Evan. 64. The liturgical notes are printed in a smaller type, for distinction.

Page 40: **'Ἀλλὰ ἡμᾶς ἐπὶ τῆς Εὐχαριστίας λέγοντας, 'εἰς τοὺς αἰῶνας τῶν αἰώων,'** κ.τ.λ. Contra Haer. lib. 1. c. 3.

Nothing can be more exquisitely precise than S. John's way of describing an *outside.*'" (John 20:11).

CHAPTER 7

CAUSES OF CORRUPTION CHIEFLY INTENTIONAL
I. HARMONISTIC INFLUENCE

It must not be imagined that all the causes of the depravation of the text of Holy Scripture were instinctive. Or that mistakes arose solely because scribes were overcome by personal infirmity, or were unconsciously the victims of surrounding circumstances. There was often more design and method in their error. They, or those who directed them, wished sometimes to 'correct' and 'improve' the copy or copies before them. And indeed occasionally they desired to make the Holy Scriptures witness to their own peculiar belief. Or they had their ideas of taste, and they did not scruple to alter passages to suit what they fancied was their enlightened judgment.

So we can trace a tendency to bring the Four Records (the Gospels) into one harmonious narrative, or at least to delete or to vary statements in one Gospel which 'appeared' to conflict with parallel statements in another. Or else, some Evangelical Diatessaron, or Harmony, or combined narrative now forgotten, exercised an influence over them. In such cases, whether consciously or not — since it is difficult always to keep designed and unintentional mistakes apart, and we must not be supposed to aim at scientific exactness in the arrangement adopted in this analysis — they were induced to adopt alterations of the pure Text.

THE LORD'S APPEARANCE TO MARY MAGDALENE

Nothing can be more exquisitely precise than S. John's way of describing an incident to which S. Mark (16:9) only refers; viz. our Lord's appearance to Mary Magdalene, the first after His Resurrection. The reason is discoverable for every word the Evangelist uses: its form and collocation. Both S. Luke (24:3) and previously S. Mark (16:5) expressly stated that the women who visited the Sepulchre on the first Easter morning, *"after they had entered in,"* saw the angels. S. John explains that at that time Mary was not with them. She had separated herself from their company, having gone in quest of Simon Peter and John. When the women had ended their visit, and in turn had departed from the Sepulchre, Mary Magdalene was left in the garden alone: *"Mary was standing* [with her face] *towards the sepulchre weeping outside."'* (John 20:11).

All this was completely misunderstood by the critics of the first two centuries. Not only did they identify the incident recorded in S. John 20:11 with that of S. Mark 15:5 and S. Luke 24:3,4 (from which S. John is careful to distinguish it) — not only did they further identify both places with S. Matt. 28:2, 3 (from which they are clearly separate) — but they considered themselves at liberty to tamper with the inspired text in order to bring it into harmony with their own erroneous convictions. Accordingly, some of them altered **πρὸς τὸ μνημεῖον** into **πρὸς τῷ μνημείῳ** (which is just as ambiguous in Greek as *'at* the sepulchre' in English). And they also boldly erased **ἔξω**. It is thus that Codex A exhibits the text. But in fact this depravation must have begun at a very remote period and prevailed to an extraordinary extent. For it disfigures the best copies of the Old Latin (the Syriac being doubtful) — a truly memorable circumstance, and in a high degree suggestive. Codes **B** reads εἰστεήκει πρὸς τῷ μνημείῳ ἔχω κλαίουσα, merely transposing (with many other authorities) the last two words. But then Codex **B** substitutes ἐλθοῦσαι for εἰσελθοῦσαι in S. Mark 16:5, in order that S. Mark may not seem to contradict S. Matt. 28:2, 3. According to this view, then, the Angelic appearance was *outside* the sepulchre. Codex **א**, on the contrary, is thorough — not only omitting ἔζω, it stands alone in reading ἐν τῷ μνημείῳ (as in the next verse **א** leaves out δύο, in order to keep S. John 20:12 from seeming to contradict S. Matt. 28:2, 3 and S. Mark 16:5). C and D do not witness here. When will men learn that these 'old uncials' are not beacon lights? Why not admit that the texts which they exhibit are not only often inconsistent, but corrupt?

There is no reason for distrusting the received reading of the present place in any particular. True, that most of the uncials and many of the cursives read πρὸς τῷ μνημείῳ, but neither Chrysostom nor Cyril so read the place. And if the Evangelist himself had so written, is it credible that a majority of the copies would have forsaken the easier and more obvious in order to exhibit the less usual and even slightly difficult expression? Many, by writing πρὸς τῷ μνημείῳ betray themselves; for they retain a sure token that the accusative ought to end the sentence. I am bent on illustrating how fatal to the purity of the Text of the Gospels has been the desire of critics to bring them into enforced agreement with one another, not understanding the inspired Gospels. I suspect that the sectional system of Eusebius is not so much the cause of the ancient and inveterate misapprehensions which prevailed in respect of the history of the Resurrection, as the consequence of them.

Luke 24:1

Those writers who overlook the corruptions which the text has experienced through a mistaken solicitude on the part of ancient critics to reconcile what seemed to them the conflicting statements of the different Evangelists, are frequently observed to attribute to this kind of officiousness expressions which are unquestionably portions of the genuine text. So there is a general consensus among critics of the destructive school to omit the words καὶ τινες συν αὐταῖς from S. Luke 24:1. Their only plea is the testimony of אBCL and certain of the Latin copies. This conjunction of authorities, when they stand alone, have before been shown to bear invariably false witness. Before we proceed to examine the evidence, we discover that these 4 words of S. Luke are even required in this place. For S. Matt. (27:61) and S. Mark (15:47) had distinctly specified two women as witnesses of how and where our Lord's body was laid. Now they were the same women apparently who prepared the spices and ointment, and who had hastened with these to the sepulchre at the break of day. If we had only S. Matthew's Gospel we would have assumed that 'the ointment-bearers' — for so the ancients called them — were but two women (28:1). But that they were at least three, even S. Mark shows by adding to their number Salome (16:1). But in fact their company consisted of more than four women, as S. Luke explains when he states that it was the same little band of holy women who had accompanied our Saviour out of Galilee (23:55; see 8:2). So in anticipation of what he will have to relate in verse 10, he says in verse 1; *"and certain with them."*

But how are we to explain the omission of these words which seem to be necessary? I answer that these words were originally ejected from the text by some because they desired to bring S. Luke's statement into harmony with that of S. Matthew, who mentions none but Mary Magdalene and Mary the mother of James and Joses. The proof is that four of the same Latin copies which are for the omission of those four words are observed to begin S. Luke 23:55 as follows: **κατακολουθήσασαι δὲ δυο γυναῖκες.** The same fabricated reading thrusting in *two* into S. Luke 23:55 is found in D. It exists also in the Codex which Eusebius employed when he wrote his Demonstratio Evangelica. So instead of wearying the reader with the evidence, which is simply overwhelming, I invite him to notice that the tables have been turned on our opponents. There is indeed found to have been a corruption of the text hereabouts, and of the words just now under discussion. But it belongs to an exceedingly remote age; and happily the record of it survives to this day only in אBCDL and certain of the Old Latin copies. How calamitous it is that Lachmann and Tregelles and Tischendorf and Alford and Westcott/Hort should so resolutely thrust out of its place words of the Sacred Text which the Church has long since deliberately refused to part with.

In S. Luke's Gospel (4:1-13) no less than six copies of the Old Latin versions, besides Ambrose in his commentary, are observed to transpose the second and third temptations; introducing verses 9-12 between verses 4 and 5 — this is in order to make the history of the Temptation as given by S. Luke to correspond with the account given by S. Matthew. The scribe of the Vercelli Codex (a) was about to do the same thing. But he checked himself when he had gotten as far as *"the pinnacle of the temple"* which he seems to have thought as good a scene for the third temptation as *"a high mountain,"* and so left it.

[See the second Appendix to *The Traditional Text* for a very interesting instance of such harmonistic influence in the substitution of *wine* for *vinegar*.]

A favorite, and certainly a plausible, method of accounting for the presence of unauthorized matter in MSS. is to suggest that at the beginning it probably existed only in the shape of a marginal note, which through the inadvertence of scribes in process of time found its way into the sacred text. Some depravations of Scripture in codices may possibly have arisen thus. But I suspect that the hypothesis is generally a wholly mistaken one, having been imported into this subject-matter from the region of the study of the Classics. For we know that the phenomenon is even common there. Especially is this hypothesis resorted to in order to explain those instances of assimilation which are so frequently to be met with in Codd. **B** and **א**.

Another favorite way of accounting for instances of assimilation is by taking for granted that the scribe was thinking of the parallel or cognate place. Certainly there is no denying that just as the familiar language of a parallel place in another Gospel presents itself unbidden to the memory of a reader, so may it have struck a copyist also with sufficient vividness to persuade him to write the words he remembered instead of the words he saw before him. All this is certainly possible.

But I suspect that this is not by any means the right way to explain the phenomena of harmonistic influence. Such depravations of the text were in the first instance intentional. I do not mean that they were introduced with any sinister motive. my meaning is that there was a desire to remove obscurities, or to reconcile what looked like incongruous passages — or generally to try to improve the style of the authors, and so to add to the merits of the sacred writings, instead of detracting from them. Such a mode of dealing with the Holy Deposit reveals a failure on the part of those who adopted this method. For they did not understand the nature of the trust committed to the Church, just as similar action at the present day does in the case of those who load the New Testament with so-called 'various readings.' These seek to illustrate it with what are really insinuations of doubt, just as they are accustomed to do when they prepare an edition of the secular Classics with the purpose of enlarging and sharpening the minds of youthful students. The intention may have been good, but it was none the less productive of corruption of the sacred text.

I suspect that if we ever obtain a specimen of those connected Gospel narratives called Diatessarons, which are known to have existed anciently in the Church, then we shall be furnished with a clue to a problem which at present is shrouded in obscurity. With our present instruments of criticism we can do no more than conjecture what was their influence. I allude to those many occasions on which the oldest documents in narrating some incident which really presents no difficulty are observed to diverge into hopeless variety of expression.

Matthew 17:25, 26

Take the incident of our Lord's paying tribute (Matt. 17:25, 26): "*And when he had entered into the house, Jesus was beforehand with him, saying, What do you think Simon? Of whom do earthly kings take toll or tribute? Of their sons or of strangers?*" Here, for ὅτε εἰσῆλθεν, Codex B (but no other uncial) substitutes ἐλθόντα; Codex ℵ, but no other, εἰσελθόντα; Codex D, but no other, εἰσελθόντι; Codex C, but no other, ὅτε ἦλθον; while a fifth lost copy certainly contained εἰσελθόντων; and a sixth, ἐλθόντων αὐτῶν. This is a fair specimen of the discordance displayed by the oldest uncials. How, then, is all this discrepancy to be accounted for?

S. Matthew proceeds: "*Peter says to Him (λέγει αὐτῷ Πέτρος), "Of strangers.*" These four words are retained by C, but continues with the addition, 'Now when he had said, Of strangers' — which unauthorized clause is found also in ℵ, except for the word αὐτοῦ. But for λέγει αὐτῷ ὁ Πέτρος ℵ alone of the uncials substitutes ὁ δέ ἔφη; and B sustibutes εἰπόντος δέ; then B proceeds exactly like the Received Text. But D merely omits ὁ Πέτρος. How can all this discrepancy be explained?[2]

I suspect that it was occasioned in the first instance by the prevalence of harmonized Gospel narratives. In no other loyal way can I account for the perpetual recurrence of such perplexing differences as we see in such documents as BℵD, Cureton's Syriac, and copies of the Old Latin version. It is well known that at a very remote period some eminent persons occupied themselves in constructing such harmonies, and also that these productions enjoyed great favor, and were in general use. As for their contents, we envision a Diatessaron as a document which aspired to be a weaving of the fourfold Gospel into one continuous narrative. And we suspect that in accomplishing this object the writer was by no means scrupulous about retaining the precise words of the inspired original. On the contrary he held himself at liberty, (a) to omit what seemed to himself to be superfluous clauses; (b) to introduce new incidents; (c) to supply picturesque details; (d) to give a new turn to the expression; (e) to vary the construction at pleasure; (f) even slightly to paraphrase. These productions compiled at a time when the preciousness of the inspired documents seem to have been imperfectly apprehended seem to have been recommended by their graphic interest, and sanctioned by a mighty name. This then was imposed on ordinary readers. Incautious owners of Codexes must have transferred without scruple certain unauthorized readings to the margins of their own copies. A calamitous partiality for the fabricated document may have prevailed with some for whom copies were executed. Above all, it is to be inferred that licentious and rash Editors of Scripture —

among whom Origen may certainly be regarded as a prime offender — must have deliberately introduced into their recensions ('translations') many an unauthorized and uninspired gloss, and so have given it an extended circulation.

Not that we would imply that permanent mischief has resulted to the Deposit from the vagaries of individuals in the earliest age. The Divine Author of Scripture has abundantly provided for the safety of His written Word by providentially protecting it in Lectionaries, in Versions, in citations by the Fathers, and in the multitude of copies of the sacred text. But then, of these multitudinous sources of protection we must not be slow to avail ourselves impartially. The prejudice which would erect Codd. B and ℵ into an imperative authority for the text of the New Testament from which they shall be no appeal —the superstitious reverence which has grown up for one little cluster of authorities to the disparagement of all other evidence wherever found — this, which is forever landing Critics in results which are simply irrational and untenable, must be unconditionally abandoned if any progress is to be made in this department of inquiry. But when this has been done, men will begin to open their eyes to the fact that the little handful of documents recently so much in favor are contrariwise the only surviving witnesses to corruptions of the Text, corruptions which the Church in her corporate capacity has long since deliberately rejected.

[As an example of the attitude of certain editors, note in Cureton's Syriac the *patch-work* supplement to S. Matt. 21:9: πολλοὶ δὲ (Mark 11:8) ἐζῆλθον εἰς ὑπάντησιν αὐτοῦ. καί (John 12:13) ἤρζαντο . . . χαίροντες αἰνεῖν τὸν Θεόν . . . περὶ πασῶν ὦιδον (Luke 19:37). This self-evident fabrication is commented on by Dr. Cureton as follows: 'if it be not a part of the original Aramaic of S. Matthew, it would appear to have been supplied from the parallel passages of Luke and John conjointly.' How is it that even a sense of humor did not preserve that eminent scholar from hazarding such a conjecture, that such a self-evident deflection of his corrupt Syriac Codex of the true Text should be pursued as if it were the recovery of a genuine utterance of the Holy Ghost?

CHAPTER 7 FOOTNOTES

Page 44: ᾽Μαρί δὲ εἰστήκει πρός τό μνημεῖον κλαίουσα ἔζω (John 20:11 Compare the expression πρός τό φῶς in Luke 22:56. Note that the above is not offered as a revised translation, but only to show unlearned readers what the words of the original exactly mean.

Page 47: ᾽I am tempted to inquire: By virtue of what verifying faculty do Lachmann and Tregelles on the former occasion adopt the reading of the Sinaiticus Codex; Tischendorf, Alford, Westcott and Hort, the reading of B? On the second occasion, I venture to ask: What enabled the Revisers, with Lachmann, Tischendorf, Tregelles, Westcott and Hort to recognize in a reading, which is the peculiar property of B, the genuine language of the Holy Ghost? Is not a superstitious reverence for B and the Sinaiticus forever betraying people into error?

CHAPTER 8

CAUSES OF CORRUPTION CHIEFLY INTENTIONAL
II. ASSIMILATION

There results inevitably from the fourfold structure of the Gospel, from the very fact that the story of the Redemption is set forth in four narratives, three of which often ran parallel, this practical inconvenience: namely, that sometimes the expressions of one Evangelist get improperly transferred to another. This is a large and important subject which calls for great attention, and which should be separately handled. The phenomena may be comprised under the special head of Assimilation. It will promote clearness in the ensuing discussion if we determine to consider separately those instances of Assimilation which may be regarded as deliberate attempts to reconcile one Gospel with another. For there are indications that in many cases there was a fixed determination to establish harmony between place and place. There are ordinary cases of Assimilation which occur in every page, and there are extraordinary instances where an enforced harmony has been established. They abound also, but are by no means common.

The whole province is beset with difficulties, and the matter is in itself wondrously obscure. In the absence of any evidence direct or indirect on the subject, it does not appear that there has been at any time one definite authoritative attempt made by the Universal Church in her corporate capacity to remodel or to revise the Text of the Gospels. An attentive study of the phenomena leads me to believe that the several corruptions of the text were effected at different times, and too their beginning in widely different ways. Accident was the parent of many; and well-meant assiduity of more. Zeal for the Truth is accountable for not a few depravations. And the Church's liturgical and lectionary practice must insensibly have produced others. Systematic villainy, I am persuaded, had no part in the matter. The decrees of such an one as Origen, if there ever was another like him, will account for a strange number of aberrations from the Truth. And if the Diatessaron of Tatian could be recovered, I suspect that we should behold there the germs of at least many more. My conviction is that however they may have originated, the causes are not to be found in bad principle, but either in infirmities or influences which actuated scribes unconsciously, or in a lack of understanding, as to what is the Church's duty in the transmission from generation to generation of the sacred Deposit.

DEFINITION AND EXAMPLES OF ASSIMILATION

When we speak of Assimilation, we do not mean that a writer while engaged in transcribing one Gospel was so completely beguiled and overpowered by his recollections of the parallel place in another Gospel that he unconsciously adopted the language which properly belonged to a different Evangelist. That this may have taken place to a very limited extent cannot be denied. But it would argue incredible inattention to what he was professing to copy, and astonishing familiarity of what he was not professing to copy. It is incredible that a scribe should have been capable of offending largely in this way. But in fact a moderate acquaintance with the subject is enough to convince any thoughtful person that the corruptions of MSS. which have resulted from accidental Assimilation must be inconsiderable, as well as few in number. At all events the phenomenon referred to when we speak of Assimilation is not to be so accounted for. It must be explained in some entirely different way.

(a) We shall probably be agreed that when the scribe of ℵ writes ἡμᾶς ἀπολέσαι in the place of Βασανίσαι ἡμᾶς (Matt. 8:29), it may have been his memory which misled him. He may have been merely thinking of S. Mark 1:24, or of S. Luke 4:34.

(b) Again when in Codd. Bℵ we find τασσόμενος thrust without warrant into S. Matt. 8:9, we see that the word has lost its way from S. Luke 7:8. And we are prone to suspect that it has crept into the parallel narrative of S. Matthew only by accident.

(c) In the same way doubtless ποταμῷ appears in BℵC, etc. in S. Matt. 3:6 because of the influence of the parallel place in S. Mark (1:5). It is astonishing that critics should have been beguiled into adopting so clear a corruption of the text as part of the genuine Gospel.

(d) The insertion by ℵ of ἀδελφέ in S. Matt. 7:4 is confessedly the result of the parallel passage in S. Luke 6:42. The same scribe may be thought to have written τῷ ἀνέμῳ in S. Matt. 8:26 only because he was so familiar with the same words in S. Luke 8:24 and in S. Mark 4:39. The author of the prototype of ℵBD — with whom are some of the Latin versions — may have written ἔχετε in S. Matt. 16:8 only because he was thinking of the parallel place in S. Mark 8:17. And ἤρξαντο ἀγανακτεῖν can only have been introduced into ℵ in S. Matt. 20:24 from the parallel place in S. Mark 10:41. S. Luke 19:21 is clearly not parallel to S. Matt. 25:24, yet it evidently furnished the scribe of ℵ with the epithet αὐστηρός in place of σκληρός. And the substitution of ℵ of ὅν παρητοῦτο in S. Matt. 27:15 for ὅν ἤθελον may seem to be the result of inconvenient familiarity with the parallel place in S. Mark 15:6, where also ℵBA viciously exhibit ὅν παρητοῦντο instead of ὅνπερ ᾐτοῦτο — which Tischendorf and Westcott/Hort mistake for the genuine Gospel. Also, who will hesitate to admit that when ℵL exhibit in S. Matt. 19:16 — instead of the words ποιήσω ἵνα ἔχω ζωὴν αἰώνιον the formula which is found in the parallel place in S. Luke 18:18, viz. ποιήσας ζωὴν αἰώνιον κληρονομήσω, and those unauthorized words must have been derived from this latter place?

(e) But I might have been disposed to admit that when ℵDL introduce into S. Matt. 10:12 the clause λέγοντες, εἰρήνη τῷ οἴκῳ τούτῳ (which last four words belong exclusively to S. Luke 10:5, the author of the depraved original from which ℵDL were derived may have been only yielding to the suggestions of an inconveniently good memory; may have succeeded in convincing himself from what follows in verse 13 that S. Matthew must have written, *"Peace be to this house;"* though he found no such words in S. Matthew's text. And so, with the best of intentions, he may most probably have inserted them.   (f) Again, when ℵ and Evan. 61 thrust into S. Matt. 9:24 the clause εἰδότες ὅτι ἀπέθανεν from the parallel place in S. Luke 8:53, it is conceivable that the authors of those copies were merely the victims of excessive familiarity with S. Luke's Gospel. But though we are ready to make every allowance for such memories, and to imagine a set of inattentive scribes open to inducements to recollect or imagine, instead of copying, and possessed of an inconvenient familiarity with one particular Gospel — it is clear that our complaisance must stop somewhere. Instances of this kind of licence at last breed suspicion. Systematic Assimilation cannot be the effect of accident. Considerable interpolations must of course be intentional. The discovery that D introduces 32 words from S. Mark 1:45-2:1 at the end of S. Luke 5:14 opens our eyes. This wholesale importation suggests an inquiry as to how it came about? Looking further we find that Cod. D abounds in instances of Assimilation so unmistakably intentional that this asks the question, How may all these depravations of the sacred text be accounted for? The answer is evidently found in the existence of extreme licentiousness in the scribe or scribes responsible for Codex D, that it is the product of ignorance and carelessness, combined with such looseness of principle as to permit the exercise of direct attempts to 'improve' the sacred Text by the introduction of passages from the three remaining Gospels, and by other alterations.

SOMETIMES THE TRUE TEXT BEARS WITNESS TO ITSELF

ℵBDL, with a few copies of the Old Latin and one of the Egyptian versions,[1] conspire in omitting from S. John 16:16 the clause ὅτι ἐγὼ ὑπάγω πρὸς τὸν Πατέρα. And so Tischendorf, Tregelles, Alford, Westcott/Hort omit those six words, and Lachmann puts them into brackets. Yet let the context be considered. Our Saviour had said in verse 16, *"A little while and you shall not see Me; and again, a little while and you shall see Me, because I go to the Father."* It follows in verse 17, *"Then said some of His disciples among themselves, What is this that He says to us, A little while and you shall not see Me; and again, a little while and you shall see me; and, Because I go to the Father?"* Now the context here, the general sequence of words and ideas, in and by itself creates a high degree of probability that the clause is genuine. At all events it must be permitted to retain its place in the Gospel unless there is found to exist an overwhelming amount of authority for its exclusion. What then are the facts? All the other uncials, headed by A and I (both of the fourth century); every known cursive; all the versions; are all for retaining the clause. Nonnus (A.D. 400) recognizes it; Chrysostom and Cyril do the same; both those Fathers and also Euthymius and Theophylact in their commentaries expressly bear witness to its genuineness. Then with what show of reason can it any longer be pretended that anyone is warranted in leaving out the words? But how did the words come to be omitted? Some early critic, no doubt, was unable to see the exquisite proprieties of the entire passage, and so thought it desirable to bring verse 16b into conformity with verse 19, where our Lord seems at first sight to resyllable the matter. That is all!

The selfsame thing has happened in verse 18, as Tischendorf candidly acknowledges, where τοῦτο τί ἐστιν has been tastelessly assimilated by BDLY to the τί ἐστιν τοῦτο which went immediately before.

John 13:21-25

I would find it difficult to lay my finger on any incident in the Gospel more apt for my purpose than the transaction described in S. John 13:21-25. It belongs to the closing scene of our Saviour's ministry: *"Verily, verily, I say to you, one of you will betray Me. Therefore the disciples looked one at another, wondering of whom He spoke. Now there was reclining in the bosom of Jesus one of His disciples whom Jesus loved. To him therefore Simon Peter motioned to inquire who it may be concerning whom He spoke. He then, just sinking on the breast of Jesus, says to Him, Lord, who is it?"* The Greek is exquisite. At first S. John has been said to be simply *reclining in the bosom* of his Divine Master. His place at the Supper is the one next to Him, for the phrase means little more. But the proximity is of course excessive, as the sequel shows. Understanding from S. Peter's gesture what is required of him,

S. John merely sinks back, allowirg his head to fall onto his Master's chest, and saying softly, *"Lord, who is it?"* The moment is perhaps the most memorable in S. John's life; the position being one of unutterable privilege. Time, place, posture, action all settle so deep into his soul that when he would identify himself in his old age, he describes himself as *"the disciple whom Jesus loved; who also at the Suppe* lay on Jesus'breast and said, Lord, who is it that is to betray Thee?"* (John 21:20). Yes, and the Church was not slow to take the beautiful hint, for his language so kindled her imagination that the early Fathers learned to speak of S. John the Divine as **ὁ ἐπιστήθιος**, 'the recliner on the chest.'

Now every delicate discriminating touch in this sublime picture is faithfully retained throughout by the cursive copies in the proportion of about eighty to one. The great bulk of the MSS., as usual, uncial and cursive alike, establish the undoubted text of the Evangelist, which here is the Received Text. Thus a vast majority of the MSS., headed by ℵAD, read **ἐπιπεσών** in S. John 13:25. Chrysostom and probably Cyril confirm the same reading, as does Nonnus. Not so B and C with four other uncials, and about twenty cursives (the vicious Evan. 33 being at their head), besides Origen in two places and apparently Theodore of Mopsuestia. These, by mischievously assimilating the place in chapter 13 to the later place in chapter 21 hopelessly obscure S. John's meaning. For they substitute **ἀναπεσών οὖν ἐκεῖνος κ.τ.λ.** It is exactly as when children by way of improving the sketch of a great Master go over his matchless outlines with a clumsy pencil of their own.

That this is the true history of the substitution of **ἀναπεσών** in St. John 13:25 for the less obvious **ἐπιπεσών** is certain. Origen, who was probably the author of all the mischief, twice sets the two places side by side and elaborately compares them. And in doing so he betrays the viciousness of the text which he himself employed. But what further helps to explain how easily **ἀναπεσών** might usurp the place of **ἐπιπεσών** is the discovery that the ancients from the earliest period were in the habit of identifying S. John by calling him 'the one that lay (**ὁ ἀναπεσών**) on the Lord's chest.' The expression, derived from S. John 21:20, is employed by Irenaeus; by Polycrates, Bishop of Ephesus A.D. 196; by Origen; and by Ephraim Syrus; Epiphanius; Palladius; Gregory of Nazianzus, and by his namesake Gregory of Nyssa; also by pseudo-Eusebius; pseudo-Caesarius and by pseudo-Chrysostom. The only wonder is that in spite of such influences, all the MSS. in the world except about twenty-six have retained the true reading.

Instructive in the meantime it is to note the handling of this word by some Critics. Lachmann, Tischendorf, Tregelles, Alford, Westcott/Hort have all in turn bowed to the authority of Cod. B and Origen. Bishop Lightfoot mistranslates and contends on the same side. Alford informs us that **ἐπιπεσών** has surreptitiously crept in 'from S. Luke 15:20 (Why should it? How could it?); **ἀναπεσών** not seeming appropriate. But on the contrary **ἀναπεσών** is the invariable and obvious expression, and **ἐπιπεσών** the unusual one; and until it has been explained it is the unintelligible word. Tischendorf read **ἐπιπεσών** in 1848, **ἀναπεσών** in 1859, and in 1869 reverts back to his first opinion, advocating with parental partiality what he had since found in Cod. ℵ. Is then the truth of Scripture aptly represented by that fitful beacon-light somewhere on the French coast, now visible, now eclipsed, now visible again?

Because in this department of study men are observed never to abandon a position until they are fairly shelled out and left without a pretext for remaining, I will show that **ἀναπεσών** is only one corrupt reading out of many others hereabouts. The proof of this statement follows. Might it not have been expected that the 'old uncials' (**אBACD**) would exhibit the entire context of such a passage as the present with tolerable accuracy? The reader is invited to attend to the results of collation of the five Codices below:

xiii. 21. — ο אB : υμιν λεγω *lr.* B.

22. — ουν BC : + οι Ιουδαιοι א: απορουντει D.

23. — δε B : + εκ אABCD : — ο B: + και D.

24. (*for* πυθεσθαι τις αν ειη + ουτος D) και λεγει αυτω, ειπε τις εστιν BC : (*for* λεγει) ελεγεν א : + και λεγει αυτω ειπε τις εστιν περι ου λεγει א.

25. (*for* επιπεσων) αναπεσων BC : — δε BC : (*for* δε) ουν אD . — ουτος אAD.

26. + ουν BC : + αυτω D : — ο B : + και λεγει אBD : + αν D : (*for* βαψας) εμβαψας AD : βαψω . . . και δωσω αυτω BC : + ψωμου (*after* ψωμιον) C : (*for* εμβαψας) βαψας D : (*for* και εμβαψας) βαψας ουν אBC : — το B : + λαμβανει και BC : Ισκαριωτου אBC : απο Καρυωτου D.

27. — τοτε א : — μετα το ψωμιον τοτε D : (*for* λεγει ουν) και λεγει D : — ο B.

In these seven verses, which resent no special difficulty to a transcriber, the Codexes in question are found to exhibit thirty-five varieties. B is responsible for twenty-eight of them (jointly or singly); א for twenty-two; C for twenty-one; D for nineteen; A for three. It is found that twenty-three words have been added to the text; fifteen substituted; fourteen taken away; and the construction has been changed four times. There is one case of senseless transposition. Simon, the father of Judas (not Iscariot) is declared by אBCD to have been called Iscariot. Even this is not all. What S. John relates concerning himself is hopelessly obscured. Also a speech is put into S. Peter's mouth which he certainly never uttered. It is not too much to say that in this confusion every delicate lineament has vanished from the Scriptural picture. So what are we to think of guides like אBCD, which are again proved to be utterly untrustworthy?

Mark 1:1, 2

The first two verses of S. Mark's Gospel have fared badly. Easy of transcription and presenting no special difficulty, they ought to have come down to us undisfigured by any serious variety of reading. On the contrary, owing to entirely different causes, either verse has experienced calamitous treatment. In Appendix IV of The Traditional Text I have proved that the clause "*son of God*" in verse 1 is beyond suspicion. Its removal from certain copies of the Gospel was originally due to heretical influence. But because Origen gave currency to the text so mutilated, it re-appears mechanically in several Fathers who are intent only on reproducing a certain argument of Origen's against the Manichees, and in this the mutilated text occurs. The same Origen is responsible to some extent, and in the same way, for the frequent introduction of Isaiah's name into verse 21 (whereas "*in the prophets*" is what S. Mark certainly wrote); but the appearance of Isaiah there in the first instance was due to quite a different cause. It is witnessed to by the Latin, Syriac, Gothic and Egyptian versions, as well as by אBDLΔ, and according to Tischendorf by nearly twenty-five cursives. Besides the following ancient writers are cited: Irenaeus, Origen, Porphyry, Titus, Basil, Serapion, Epiphanius, Severianus, Victor, Eusebius, Victorinus, Jerome and Augustine. I shall show that this imposing array of authorities for reading "in Isaiah the prophet' instead of *"in the prophets,"* in S. Mark 1:2 has either been overestimated, or else misunderstood.

1. The testimony of the oldest versions, when attention is paid to their contents, is discovered to be of inferior moment in minuter matters of this nature. Thus, copies of the Old Latin version thrust Isaiah's name into S. Matt. 1:22, and Zechariah's name into 21:4; as well as thrusting out Jeremiah's name from 27:9 — the first with Curetonian, Lewis, Harkleian, Palestinian, and D — the second with Chrysostom and Hilary — the third with the Peshitto. The Latin and Syriac further substitute 'the prophet' for *"the prophets"* in S. Matt. 2:23, through misapprehension of the Evangelist's meaning. What is to be thought of the Sinaiticus Codex for introducing the name of Isaiah into S. Matt. 13:35, where it clearly cannot stand (since the quotation is from Psalm 78:2). Yet Porphyry, Eusebius and pseudo-Jerome found it in many ancient copies.

2. Next, for the testimony of the uncials ℵBDLΔ, if anyone will be at the pains to tabulate the 900 new 'readings' adopted by Tischendorf in editing S. Mark's Gospel, he will discover that for 450 — all the 450 I believe to be corruptions of the text — BℵL are responsible. Further, their responsibility is shared on about 200 occasions by D; on about 265 by C; on about 350 by Δ. At some very remote period, therefore, there must have grown up a vicious general reading of S. Mark's Gospel, which remains in the few bad copies — but in which the largest traces still survive in ℵBCDLΔ (and very discreditable traces they are). After this discovery it will not be extraordinary that I regard with unmingled suspicion readings which are exclusively vouched for by these same five codexes.[2]

3. The cursive copies which exhibit Isaiah instead of *"the prophet"* which Tischendorf reckons to be 'nearly twenty-five copies,' are probably less than fifteen, and most of those of a suspicious character.[3]

4. From Tischendorf's list of thirteen Fathers, serious deductions must be made. Irenaeus and Victor of Antioch are clearly with the Received Text. Serapion, Titus and Basil only are borrowing from Origen, reproducing along with his argument his corrupt text of S. Mark 1:2. However Basil saves his reputation by leaving out the quotation from Malachi; so, passing directly from the mention of Isaiah to the actual words of that prophet. Epiphanius, and Jerome, too, does the same thing. Victorinus and Augustine, being Latin writers, merely quote the Latin version, which is without variety of reading. So Origen remains (the faulty character of his Codexes has been often pointed out,) with Porphyry the heretic (who wrote a book to convict the Evangelists of misstatements, and who therefore can hardly be viewed as a trustworthy witness); Eusebius, Jerome in another place, and Severianus. Of these Eusebius and Jerome deliver it as their opinion that the name of Isaiah had been admitted into the text through the inadvertency of copyists. Then is it reasonable, on the slender residuum of evidence, to insist that S. Mark had ascribed to Isaiah words confessedly written by Malachi? A recent editor writes, 'The fact will not fail to be observed by the careful and honest student of the Gospels' — but what if *the fact* claimed by that critic proves only to be *a fiction?* Would not his 'carefulness' be better employed in scrutinizing the adverse testimony; and his 'honesty' in admitting that on grounds as precarious as the present no indictment against S. Mark can be seriously maintained (much less confidently claimed to be 'a fact').

The Church in her corporate capacity has steadfastly refused to sanction, for the Evangelistaria know nothing of it; for it carries on its face its own sufficient condemnation. Why, in the face of all the copies in the world except a little handful of suspicious character) will men insist on imputing to an inspired writer a foolish misstatement? Why not frankly admit that the text must have been corrupted in that little handful of copies through the officiousness of incompetent criticism?

And do any inquire, How then did this perversion of the truth arise? I answer, in the easiest way possible. Refer to the Eusebian tables, and note that the foremost of his sectional parallels is as follows: S. Matthew, ἡ (i. e. 3:3) — S. Mark, Β (i. e. 1:3) — S. Luke z (i.e. 3:3-6)— S. John ί (i.e. 1:23).

Now since the name of Isaiah occurs in the first, the third and the fourth of these places in connection with the quotation from Isa. 40:3, *what* more obvious than that some critic with harmonistic proclivities should have insisted on supplying *the second also* (that is, the parallel place in S. Mark's Gospel) with the name of the prophet which is so familiarly connected with the passage quoted in other places? This is nothing else but an ordinary instance of Assimilation, so unskilfully effected as to betray itself. It might have been passed by with a few words, the fraud being so transparent, but that it is being imposed upon us by learned men, who have established it so firmly in books.

Regarded as an instrument of criticism, Assimilation requires to be very delicately as well as very skilfully handled. If it is to be applied to determining the text of Scripture, it must be employed in a very different spirit than that displayed by Dr. Tischendorf's notes; else it will but mislead. if a word, a phrase, a sentence, is omitted by his favorite authorities ℵBDL, then he will search for the same word, or a very similar clause, or a sentence of the same general import in the account of another Evangelist — then he will insist that that word, or clause, or sentence has been imported into the commonly received Text from such a parallel place; and forthwith will reject the Received Text reading.

But as the thoughtful reader must see, this is not allowable, except under peculiar circumstances. For first, whatever *a priori* improbability might be supposed to attach to the existence of identical expressions in two Evangelical records of the same transaction, is effectually disposed of by the discovery that very often identity of the expression actually does occur. Secondly, the only condition which could warrant the belief that there has been assimilation is invariably seen to be away from Dr. Tischendorf's instances — viz., a sufficient number of respectable attesting witnesses. For it is a fundamental principle in the law of Evidence that the very few are rather to be suspected than the many. Thirdly, if there is some marked diversity of expression in the two parallel places; and if that diversity has been carefully maintained all down the ages in either place — then it may be regarded as certain that there has not been assimilation — it is only one more instance of two Evangelists saying similar things, or the same thing in slightly different language.

For example, take the following case: S. Matt. (24:15) speaks of '*the abomination of desolation* τὸ ῥηθὲν διὰ Δανιὴλ τοῦ προπήτου ἑστώς standing in the holy place. But S. Mark (13:14) has it: τὸ ῥηθὲν υπο Δανιὴλ τοῦ προφήτου standing (ἑστός) where it ought not." Now because ℵBDL with copies of the Italic, the Vulgate and the Egyptian versions omit from S. Mark's Gospel the six words written above in Greek, Tischendorf and his school are for expunging those six words from S. Mark's text, pleading that they are probably an importation from S. Matthew. But the little note of variety which the

Holy Spirit has set on the place in S. Mark's Gospel (**υπο** instead of **δια**) suggests that these learned men are mistaken. Accordingly, the other fourteen uncials and all the cursives, besides the Peshitto, Harkleian, and copies of the Old Latin — a much more weighty body of evidence — are certainly right in retaining the words in S. Mark 13:14.

Take two more instances of misuse of assimilation in criticism: S. Matthew (12:10) and S. Luke (14:3) the parallel place in his Gospel, describe our Lord as asking: *"Is it lawful to heal on the sabbath day?"* Finding that his favorite authorities in S. Luke continue the sentence with the words 'or not,' Tischendorf assumes that those two words must have fallen out of the bulk of the copies of S. Luke, which according to him have here been assimilated to the phraseology of S. Matthew. But the hypothesis is clearly inadmissible, though most modern critics admit it. Do not these learned persons see that the supposition is just as lawful, and the probability infinitely greater, that it is the few copies which have here undergone the process of assimilation — that the type to which they have been conformed is to be found in S. Matt. 22:17; S. Mark 12:14 and S. Luke 20:22?

It is surprising how often a familiar place of Scripture has exerted this kind of assimilating influence over a little handful of copies. So some critics are agreed in rejecting the proposal of אBDLR to substitute for **γεμίσαι τὴν κοιλίαν αὐτοῦ ἀπό** in S. Luke 15:16 the words **χορτασθῆναι ἐκ**. But editors have omitted to point out that the words **ἐπεθύμει χορτασθῆναι**, introduced in defiance of the best authorities into the parable of Lazarus (16:20), have simply been transplanted there out of the parable of the prodigal son.

The reader has now been presented with several examples of Assimilation. Tischendorf, who habitually overlooks Assimilation where it seems to be sufficiently conspicuous, is observed constantly to discover cases of Assimilation where none exist. In fact this is his habitual way of accounting for not a few of the omissions in Cod. א. And because he has deservedly enjoyed a great reputation, it becomes the more necessary for the reader to be on his guard against receiving such statements without a thorough examination of the evidence on which they rest.

THE VALUE OF DETAILED STUDY OF ASSIMILATION

The value — may I not say, the use — of these delicate differences of detail becomes apparent whenever the genuineness of the text is called in question. Take an example:

The following fifteen words are deliberately excluded from S. Mark's Gospel (6:11) by some critics on the authority of אBCDLΔ — a most suspicious company — plus three cursives; besides a few copies of the Old Latin, including the Vulgate: **ἀμὴν λέγω ὑμῖν, ἀνεκτότερον ἔσται Σοδόομοις ἤ Γομόρροις ἐν ἡμέρᾳ κρίσεως, ἤ τῇ πόλει ἐκείνῃ** — it is pretended that this is but an importation from the parallel place of S. Matt. 10:15. But that is impossible. For, as the reader sees at a glance, a delicate but decisive note of discrimination has been set on the two places. S. Mark writes, **ΣοδομΟΙΣ ἤ ΓομόρρΟΙΣ**; whereas S. Matthew, **γῇ ΣοδόμΩΝ ΚΑΙ ΓομόρρΩΝ**. And this fourfold diversity of expression has existed from the beginning; for it has been faithfully retained all down the ages — it exists to this hour in every known copy of the Gospel, except of course those nine which omit the sentence altogether. There can be no doubt about its genuineness. The modern critics (Lachmann, Tischendorf, Tregelles, Alford,

Westcott/Hort) seek in vain to put on us a mutilated text by omitting those fifteen words. The two places are clearly independent of each other. The exclusion of these fifteen words from S. Mark 6:11 has resulted merely from the influence of the parallel place in S. Luke 9:5, where nothing whatever is found corresponding to either S. Matt. 10:15 or S. Mark 6:11. The process of Assimilation therefore has been at work here, but not in the way which these critics suppose. It has resulted, *not* in the insertion of the words in dispute into the multitude of copies, *but* on the contrary in their omission from the very few. And so one more brand of untrustworthiness is set on אBCDLΔ and their Latin allies — they *never* are found to conspire together exclusively except to mislead.

Mark 14:70

Because five more words are absent from S. Mark (14:70) in Codd. אBCDL, the modern-day critics entirely reject these five precious words: **καὶ ἡ λαλιά σου ὁμοιάζει.** Griesbach had already voted them as 'probably spurious.' When it has been added that many copies of the Old Latin, together with the Vulgate and the Egyptian versions, besides Eusebius, ignore their existence, we scarcely expect to be listened to when we insist that the words are perfectly genuine.

1. Even if the whole of the case were already before the reader, and although there might seem to exist a *prima facie* probability that the clause is spurious, yet it should not be difficult to convince a thoughtful person that the reverse must be nearer the truth. For let the parallel places in the first two Gospels be noted: S. Matthew has, **Ἀληθῶς καὶ σύ**; S. Mark has, **Ἀληθῶς.** Then S. Matthew has, **ἐξ αὐτῶν εἶ**; while S. Mark has, **ἐξ αὐτῶν εἶ.** Then S. Matthew has, **καὶ γάρ**; while S. Mark has, **καὶ γὰρ Γαλιλαῖος εἶ.** Lastly, S. Matthew has, **ἡ λαλιά σου δῆλόν σε ποιεῖ**; while S. Mark has, **καὶ ἡ λαλιά σου ὁμοιάζει** — what is more clear than that S. Mark is explaining what S. Matthew meant by *"your speech betrays you"*? Or else he is giving an independent account of the same transaction, derived from the common source. To S. Matthew (a Jew addressing Jews) it seemed superfluous to state that it was the peculiar accent of Galilee which betrayed Simon Peter. To S. Mark (or rather to the readers whom S. Mark addressed) the point was by no means so obvious. So he reveals the reason for the charge: *"for you are a Galilean and your speech corresponds."* Let me be shown that all down the ages, in ninety-nine copies out of a hundred, that this peculiar diversity of expression has been retained, and instead of assenting to the suppression of S. Mark's words, with its unique verb **ὁμοιάζει**, and I immediately take myself to the more pertinent inquiry: What is the state of the text hereabouts? What is the context? This is not a matter of opinion, but a matter of fact:

1. First, Cod D. in concert with several copies of the Old Latin only removes the last clause from its proper place in S. Mark's Gospel in order to thrust it into S. Matthew 26:73. But there it supplants *"your speech makes you manifest"* to make room for the imported clause from S. Mark. The object of D is apparently to assimilate the two Gospels, for D also omits **καὶ σύ** in the first clause.

2. The Ethiopic version, on the contrary, is for assimilating S. Mark to S. Matthew, for it transfers *"your speech makes you manifest"* from S. Matthew to S. Mark.

3. Evan. 33 (styled 'Queen of the Cursives' by those who love its reflection of the text of **B**) is more brilliant here than usual, exhibiting S. Mark's clause thus: **καὶ γὰρ ἡ λαλιά σου δῆλόν σε ὁμοιάζει.**

4. In C and in the Harkleian version the process of Assimilation is as conspicuous as in D, for it imports from S. Mark into S. Matthew the clause, *"For you are a Galilean."* C. also omits from S. Mark, *"and your speech agrees."*

5. In the Vercelli Codex (a) however, the converse process is conspicuous. S. Mark has been assimilated to S. Matthew by the unauthorized insertion of **καὶ σὺ** at the beginning of the verse (also found in M,) and with the Gothic and Evann. 73, 131, 142* entirely leaving out the clause, *"for you are a Galilean."*

6. Cod. L goes beyond all by further obliterating all trace of *"your speech makes you manifest"* from S. Matthew, and also *"for your speech agrees"* from S. Mark.

7. א and **B** alone of the Codexes, though in agreement with the Vulgate and the Egyptian versions, do only eliminate from S. Mark *"for your speech agrees."*

8. But note that Cod. A, together with the Syriac versions, the Gothic, the whole body of the cursives, recognizes none of these irregularities, but exhibits the commonly received text with entire fidelity.

Will any serious student of these premises contend now that *"for your speech agrees"* is no part of the genuine text of S. Mark 14:70? The words are found in what are virtually the most ancient authorities extant, the Syriac versions, the Old Latin (besides Cod. D), in the Gothic and Cod. A. Is it not clearly in the face of such evidence that some would pretend that S. Mark cannot have written the words in question? It is too late to insist that a man cannot have lost his watch, it having been proven that it was in his pocket at eight o'clock, and then found in another man's pocket at nine. As for C and L, their handling of the text hereabout clearly disqualifies them from being cited in evidence. They are condemned under the note of Context. Adverse testimony is borne by **B** and א, and by them only. They omit the words in dispute, an ordinary habit of omission being proven on them a host of times. But how is the punctual insertion of the words in every other known copy to be explained? Take note of Scrivener's remarks: "we have a set of passages which bear clear marks of *wilful* and critical correction, thoroughly carried out in Cod. א and only partially in Cod. **B**, and some of its compeers; the object being so far to assimilate the narrative of Peter's denials with those of the other Evangelists, as to suppress the fact, vouched for by S. Mark only, that the cock crowd twice" — Full Collation of Cod. Sinaiticus, etc., 2nd ed. p. xlvii. *That* incident shall be treated of separately. But can those principles stand, as revealed in the foregoing statement of Scrivener, and in the face of the evidence preceding it, then justify the disturbance of the text in S. Mark 14:70?

CHAPTER 8 FOOTNOTES

Page 50: 'The alleged evidence of Origen (iv. 453) is *nil*; the sum of it being that he takes no notice whatever of the forty words between **ὄψεσθέ με** (in ver. 16), and **τοῦτο τί ἐστιν** (in ver. 18).

Page 54: **אBL** are *exclusively* responsible on 45 occasions; C on 27; D on 35; Δ on 73; CD on 19; cΔ on 118; DΔ on 42; CDΔ on 66.

Page 54: 'In the text of Evan. 72 the reading in dispute is *not* found; 205, 206 are duplicates of 209; and 222, 255 are only fragments. There remain 1, 22, 33, 61, 63, 115, 131, 151, 152, 161, 184, 209, 253, 372, 391; of which the six at Rome require to be re-examined.

CHAPTER 9

CAUSES OF CORRUPTION CHIEFLY INTENTIONAL
III. ATTRACTION

Not a few corrupt readings have arisen from nothing else but the proneness of words standing side by side in a sentence to be attracted into a likeness of ending — whether in respect of grammatical form or of sound — by which sometimes the sense is made to suffer grievously; and sometimes to disappear altogether. This may be called the error of Attraction. It is quite different from Assimilation. A gross instance of this has imposed on learned critics and on our Revisers in S. John 6:71 and 13:26.

"Judas Iscariot" is a combination of appellatives with which every Christian ear is familiar. The expression is found in S. Matt. 10:4; 26:14; S. Mark 3:19; 14:10; S. Luke 6:16; 22:31, with the express statement added that Judas was so *"surnamed."* S. John's invariable practice is to designate the traitor, whom he names four times, as *"Judas Iscariot, the son of Simon;"* no doubt jealous for the honor of his brother apostle, Jude, the brother of James; and resolved that there should be no mistake about the traitor's identity. Who does not recall S. John's striking parenthesis in S. John 14:22, *"Judas, not Iscariot"*? Accordingly, in S. John 13:3 the Revisers present us with *"Judas Iscariot, Simon's son;"* and even in S. John 12:4 they are content to read *"Judas Iscariot."*

But in two places of S. John's Gospel (6:71 and 13:26) instead of *"Judas Iscariot the son of Simon,"* the Revisers require us to read, 'Judas the son of Simon ISCARIOT.' Why? It is only because in place of 'Ιούδαν 'ΙσκαριώTHN (in 6:71) and 'Ιούδạ Σίμονος 'ΙσκαριώTΗ (in 13:26)—a little handful of copies substitute in both places 'ΙσκαριώTOY. Need I go on? Nothing else evidently happened but that, through the drowsiness of an early scribe, the 'ΙσκαριώTHN, 'ΙσκαριώTΗ, have been attracted into concord with the immediately preceding *genitive* ΣΙμωΝΟΣ ... so transparent a blunder would have scarcely deserved a passing remark at our hands if it had not been allowed to remain in the columns of Codd. **B** and **ℵ**. But not only have the Revisers adopted this corrupt reading in both passages, but they have not left so much as a hint that any alteration has been made in the inspired Text.

Another far graver case of Attraction is found in Acts 20:24. In his address to the elders of Ephesus S. Paul refers to the discouragements he had encountered: *"But none of these things move me,"* he grandly exclaims, *"neither do I count my life dear to myself, so that I might finish my course with joy."* The Greek for this begins ἀλλ' οὐδενὸς λόγον ποιοῦμαι — but some second or third century copyist was misled by the preceding genitive, and in place of λόγοΝ he wrote λόγοΥ; with what calamitous consequence we explained before. Happily the error survives only in Codd. **B** and C; and their bad character has already been demonstrated many times.

In a certain place (2 Cor. 3:3) S. Paul tells the Corinthians that they are an epistle not written on *stony tables,* but on *fleshy tables of the heart"* (alluding to the language of Exodus 31:12 and 34:1). The one proper proof that this is what S. Paul wrote is not only (1) that the copies largely preponderate in favor of so exhibiting the place; but, (2) that the versions, with the single exception of the Harkleian, are all on the same side: and lastly, (3) that the Fathers are as nearly as possible unanimous. Let the evidence for **καρδίας** (unknown to Tischendorf and the rest) be produced in detail: In the second century, Irenaeus; the Old Latin; the Peshitto. In the third century, Origen seven times; the Coptic version.

In the fourth century, the Dialogus; Didymus; Basil; Gregory of Nyssa; Marcus the Monk; Chrysostom in two places; Nilus; the Vulgate; and the Gothic versions.

In the fifth century, Cyril; Isidorus; Theodoret; the Armenian and Ethiopic.

In the seventh century, Victor, Bishop of Carthage addressing Theodorus P.

In the eighth century, J. Damascene; and of the Latins, Hilary; Ambrose; Optatus; Jerome; Tichonius; Augustine thirteen times; Fulgentius; and others.

If this is not overwhelming evidence, may I be told what is?[4]

But it so happens a surprising number of copies are found to exhibit the 'perfectly absurd' and 'wholly unnatural' reading: **πλαξί καρδιΑΙΣ σαρκινΑΙΣ**, having been attracted by the two datives between which **καρδίας** stands, and tempted by the consequent jingle of it. And because A[1], BℵCD, one and all adopt the false reading — Lachmann, Tischendorf, Tregelles, Alford and Westcott/Hort advocate this awkward blunder — as do the Revisers of 1881, without so much as a hint in the margin that the evidence is overwhemingly against themselves, and in favor of the traditional Text.

That I may not be accused of suppressing what is to be said on the other side, the sum of the adverse evidence (besides those uncials) is the Harkleian version; the doubtful testimony of Eusebius; Cyril in one place; and lastly a quotation from Chrysostom on the Maccabees, given in Cramer's Catena, vii. 595, which reappears at the end of eight lines without the word **πλαξι**.

CHAPTER 9 FOOTNOTES

Page 60: [1]Yet strange to say, Tischendorf claims the support of Didymus and Theodoret on **καρδίας**, on the ground that in the course of their expository remarks they contrast **καρδίαι σάρκιναι** (or **λογικαί**) with **πλάκες λίθιναι** — as if it were not the word **πλαξί** which alone occasions difficulty. Again, Tischendorf enumerates Cod. E (Paul) among his authorities. Had he then then forgotten that E is *nothing better than a transcript of D* (Claromontanus), made by some ignorant person? Also that 'the Greek is *manifestly worthless*, and that it should long since have been removed from the list of authorities?' (Scrivener's Intro., 4th ed., i. 177). See Also the note in *The Traditional Text*. Tischendorf is frequently inaccurate in his references to the Fathers also.

CHAPTER 10

CAUSES OF CORRUPTION CHIEFLY INTENTIONAL
IV. OMISSION

Now we must consider the largest of all classes of corrupt variations from the genuine Text (these are empirical, not logical classes) — the omission of words, clauses and sentences. This is truly a fertile province of inquiry. Omissions are much in favor with a particular school of critics; though a habit of admitting omissions, whether in ancient or modern times, cannot but be symptomatic of a tendency to skepticism.

Omissions are often treated as 'various readings.' Yet only by an Hibernian licence can words omitted be so reckoned. For in truth the very essence of the matter is that on such occasions *nothing* is read. It is to the case of words omitted that this chapter is to be exclusively devoted. Bear in mind that I speak now of those words alone where the words are observed to exist in ninety-nine MSS. out of a hundred; that is, missing only from that hundredth copy.

Now it becomes evident as soon as attention has been called to the circumstance that such a phenomenon as omission requires separate treatment. Words omitted labor *prima facie* under a disadvantage which is all their own. My meaning will be best illustrated by a few examples:

The most crucial case and most conspicuous within the whole compass of the New Testament is the omission of the last twelve verses of S. Mark's Gospel, often bracketed off, or else entirely severed from the rest of the Gospel by Critics. For full and complete defense of these verses, see elsewhere in this volume the full-size book, a book that has never been refuted by anyone at any time.

We have already seen enough of the character of the modern-day Critics, those who are blinded by invincible prejudice in favor of those unsafe guides B and ℵ, and on behalf of omissions. Now what is there about omissions that lend themselves to acceptance to these minds? We can imagine nothing except the halo which they have placed around the detection of spurious passages in modern times, and has been extended to a *supposed* detection of passages which in fact *are not spurious*. Some people appear to feel delight if they can 'prove' any charge against people who claim to be orthodox; others delight in 'superior' criticism, with or without delight. And also the flavor of scepticism especially commends itself to the taste of many. To the devotees of such criticism, omission of passages which they like to style 'interpolations' offer tempting hunting fields.

Yet the experience of copyists would pronounce omission to be the besetting fault of transcribers. It is so easy under the influence of the desire to accomplish a task, or at least of anxiety for making progress, to pass over a word, or a line, or even more lines than one. The eye will readily move from one ending to a similar ending with a surprising tendency to pursue the course which would lighten labor. The cumulative result of such abridgment by omission may be easily imagined. In fact, just take what can be seen in Cod. B.[1]. Besides these considerations, the passages which are omitted, and which we claim to be genuine, bear in themselves the character belonging to the rest of the Gospels — to use Dr. Hort's expressive phrase, these 'have the ring of genuineness.' These omissions are not like some of the interpolations which some critics of the same school would fain force upon us.[2] But beyond all — an this is the real source and ground of attestation — the genuine words enjoy superior evidence from copies, generally beyond comparison with the opposing testimony, and from Versions and from the early Fathers.

The fact seems to be all but overlooked that a very much larger amount of proof than usual is required at the hands of those who would persuade us to cancel words which have been regarded as inspired Scripture in all ages, in all countries, by all persons. These Critics must, (1) account for the fact that these words exist; and next, (2) must demonstrate that they have no right to their place in the sacred page. The discovery that from a few copies they are away clearly has very little to do with the question. We may be able to account for the omission from those few copies. And the instant that we have done this, the negative evidence — the argument from silence — has been effectually disposed of. A very different task; a far graver responsibility; is imposed on those advocating deletion of words from the traditional text. They must establish many modes of accounting for many classes and groups of evidence. Broad and sweeping measures are now out of date. The burden of proof lies with them.

SOME SPECIMENS OF UNAUTHORIZED OMISSIONS

The force of what I am saying will be best understood if a few actual specimens of omission may be adduced and individually considered.

First, take the case of an omitted word from S. Luke 6:1, δευτεροπρώτῳ, which is omitted from some manuscripts. Westcott/Hort and the Revisers delete this word from the text. Now I desire to be informed how it is credible that so very difficult and peculiar a word as this — for the expression has never yet been satisfactorily explained — should have found its way into every known Evangelium except אBL and a few cursives, if it is indeed spurious? How it came to be here and there omitted is intelligible enough. But glance at Cod. א:

ΤΟ ΕΝ ΣΑΒΒΑΤΩ
ΔΕΥΤΕΡΟΠΡΩΤΩ

Note the like ending of these two lines (ΤΩ) — the scribe's eyes simply skipped over the second line. (b) A proper lectionary lesson begins at this place; which by itself would explain the phenomenon. (c) Words which copyists were at a loss to understand are often observed to be dropped; and there is no harder word in the Gospel than this word. Now will you tell us how it is conceivable that a word nowhere else found, and known to be a *crux* to commentators and others, should have crept into all the copies except a small handful?

In reply to this, I shall be told that really I must yield to what is after all the *weight* of external evidence; that Codd. אBL are not *ordinary* MSS., but 'first-class authorities, of sufficient importance to outweigh any number of the later cursive MSS.

My rejoinder is plain: Not only am I willing to yield to external evidence, but it is precisely this external evidence which makes me insist on retaining δευτεροπρώτῳ; and the genuineness of S. Matt. 23:14; and the authenticity of the last twelve verses of Mark. I entirely deny the cogency of the proposed proof, and have clearly already established the grounds of my refusal. Who then is to be the daysman between us? We are driven back to first principles in order to ascertain if it may not be possible to meet on some common ground. By the application of ordinary logical principles of reasoning we can clear our view.

[The reader is referred to *The Traditional Text* portion of this volume to gain Dean Burgon's principles and logic. There various cases of omission have been discussed, and evidence given. Here he gives specimens of more omissions.]

Matthew 21:44

Fifteen words of the 44th verse of S. Matt. 21 is marked as doubtful by Tregelles, Westcott/Hort and the Revisers; and Tischendorf rejects them as spurious.[3] We insist that these words are without doubt genuine; reasoning from antiquity, variety, respectability, largeness, and the general unanimity of the attestation. For the verse is found in the Old Latin, and in the Vulgate, the Peshitto, the Curetonian and Harkleian Syriac, besides the Coptic, Armenian, and Ethiopic versions. It is found in Origen, ps.-Tatian, Aphraates, Chrysostom, Cyril Alex., the Opus Imperfectum, Jerome, Augustine of the Fathers. They are found in BℵCΦXZΔΠEFGHKLMSUV — in short they are attested by every known Codex except two of bad character (D and 33, with five copies of the Old Latin). There have therefore been adduced for the verse in dispute at least five witnesses of the second or third century; at least eight of the fourth; at least seven if not eight of the fifth; after which date the testimony is simply overwhelming. How could anyone be justified in opposing to such a mass of first-rate testimony since the solitary evidence of Cod. D is supported only by a single errant cursive and a little handful of copies of the Old Latin versions? however, it is joined by the Lewis Codex?

But Tischendorf says that the verse is omitted by Origen and by Eusebius; by Iranaeus, and by Lucifer of Cagliari; as well as by Cyril of Alexandria. I answer that this most insecure of arguments for mutilating the traditional text is plainly inadmissible on the present occasion. The Critic refers to the fact that Iranaeus, Origen, Eusebius and Cyril, having quoted 'the parable of the wicked husband-men extensively (from verse 33 to verse 43) *leave off at verse 43*. And why may they not leave off where the parable leaves off? Why quote any further? Verse 44 has no relationship to the parable. And since the Gospel for Monday morning in Holy Week deals with verses 18 through 43 in every known copy of the Lectionary, actually ending at verse 43 — why should not verse 43 be the end of their quotations? But, unfortunately for Dr. Tischendorf's claim, Origen and Cyril elsewhere actually quote the verse he is spurning. And how can Tischendorf maintain that Lucifer yields adverse testimony? That Father quotes *nothing but* verse 43, which is all that he requires for his purpose. Why should he have quoted verse 44? Macarius Egyptius and Philo of Carpasus also quote only verse 43, yet this is not evidence that they thought verse 44 to be spurious.

Tischendorf's opinion that this verse is a fabricated imitation of the parallel verse in S. Luke (20:18) is clearly untenable. Either place has its distinctive type, both having been maintained intact all down the ages. The single fact that S. Matt. 21:44 has a sectional number to itself in the Peshitto version is far too weighty to be set aside on nothing better than suspicion. *If a verse so elaborately attested as this one is not genuine, then we must abandon all hope of ever attaining to any certainty concerning the Text of Scripture!*

In the meantime there emerges from the treatment which S. Matt. 21:44 has experienced at the hands of Tischendorf the discovery that, in his estimation, Cod. D is a document of so much importance that it can occasionally outweigh almost all other evidence, even all the other copies of all ages and countries.

Matthew 15:8

My next example is a deliberate choice in order to refute the peculiar theory of Textual Revision which Dr. Tregelles advocates so strenuously. Since the days of Griesbach this theory has enjoyed the absolute confidence of most of the illustrious editors of the New Testament. This one is in fact the second example on Dr. Tregelles' list. I take leave to point out that Dr. Tregelles unintentionally hoodwinks his readers by not setting before them in full the problem which he proposes to discuss. To thoroughly understand this matter, the student should be reminded that there are two parallel verses, one in S. Matthew 15:8; the other in S. Mark 7:6:

Matthew 15:8	Mark 7:6
"Hypocrites, well did Isaiah prophesy of you saying, 'This people draws nigh unto Me with their mouth and honors Me with their lips (ἐγγίζει μοι ὁ λαὸς οὗτος τῷ στόματι αὐτῶν, καὶ τοῖς χείλεσί με τιμᾷ), but their heart is far from Me.'"	"Well did Isaiah prophesy of you, hypocrites, as it is written, 'This people honors Me with their lips (οὗτος ὁ λαὸς τοῖς χείλεσί με τιμᾷ), but their heart is far from Me.'"

The place referred to is Isaiah 29:13, which reads as follows in the Septuagint: καὶ εἶπε κύριος, ἐγγίζει μοι ὁ λαὸς οὗτος ἐν τῷ στόματι αὐτοῦ, καὶ ἐν τοῖς χείλεσιν αὐτῶν τιμῶσί με.

Now about the text of S. Mark in this place no question is raised. Nor is there any 'various reading' worth speaking of in ninety-nine out of a hundred MSS. in respect of the text in S. Matthew. But when reference is made to the two oldest copies in existence, Bℵ, we are presented with what would have appeared to be a strangely abbreviated reading, if it were not for the parallel place in S. Mark. Both B and ℵ conspire in exhibiting S. Matt. 15:8 as follows: ὁ λαὸς οὗτος τοῖς χείλεσί με τιμᾷ — leaving out six words (ἐγγίζει μοι and τῷ στόματι αὐτῶν, καὶ). They are joined in this peculiarity by DLT, two cursives, and the following versions: Old Latin, except f; Vulgate; Curetonian; Lewis; Peshitto and Bohairic. Cod. A, the Sahidic and Gothic versions, are imperfect here and so cannot testify. To this evidence Tischendorf adds a phalanx of Fathers: Clemens Romanus (A.D. 70); Ptolemaeus the Gnostic (A.D. 150); Clemens Alex. (A.D. 190); Origen in three places (A.D. 210); Eusebius; Basil, Cyril of Alex.; Chrysostom. Alford also supplies Justin Martyr (A.D. 150). The testimony of Didymus, which has been hitherto overlooked, is express. Tertullian, Cyprian, Hilary are naturally found to follow the Latin copies. Such a weight of evidence may not unreasonably inspire Dr. Tregelles with an exceeding amount of confidence. Accordingly he declares, 'that this one passage might be relied on as an important proof that it is the few MSS. and not the many which accord with ancient testimony.' Availing himself of Dr. Scrivener's admission of 'the possibility that the disputed words in the great bulk of the MSS. were inserted from the Septuagint of Isaiah 29:13;' Dr. Tregelles insists 'that on every true principle of textual criticism the words must be regarded as an amplification borrowed from the Prophet. This naturally explains their introduction.' Then he adds, 'and when once they had gained a footing in the text, it is certain that they would be multiplied by copyists, who almost always preferred to make passages as full and complete as possible.' (p. 139). Dr. Tregelles therefore relies on this one passage — not so much as a 'proof that it is the few MSS. and not the many which accord with ancient testimony' — for one instance cannot possible prove *that*; and that is after all beside the real question — but he is relying on this passage as a proof that the text of Bℵ in this place is genuine, and the text of all the other Codexes in the world are corrupt.

Now the reader has the hypothesis fully before him, one which from the days of Griesbach has been proposed to account for the discrepancy between 'the few copies' on the one hand, and the whole torrent of manuscript evidence on the other.

Now since I am writing a book on the *principles* of Textual Criticism, I must be allowed to set the reader on guard against all such unsupported dicta as the preceding — though enforced with emphasis, and recommended by a deservedly respected name. I venture to think that the exact reverse will be found to be a vast deal nearer the truth: that is that undoubtedly spurious readings may be observed to die out speedily, although they may have succeeded in obtaining a footing in MSS. at one time or the other. Seldom do they leave any considerable number of descendants. In fact there has always been a process of elimination going on, as well as one of self-propagation — a corrective force at work, as well as one of deterioration. How else are we to account for the utter disappearance of the many monstrous lections which the ancients insist were prevalent in their times?

We are invited then to believe that from the fifth century downwards *every extant copy of the Gospels except five* (DLT, 33, 124) exhibits a text arbitrarily interpolated in order to bring it into conformity with the Greek version of Isaiah 29:13. On this wild hypothesis, note the following observations:

1. It is altogether unaccountable, if this is indeed a true account of the matter, how it has come to pass that in no single MS. in the world, so far as I am aware, has this conformity been successfully achieved; for the Evangelical Text differs from the Septuagintal reading of Isaiah 29:13 no less than six ways.

2. Further, if there really did exist this strange determination of the ancients to assimilate the text of S. Matthew to the text of Isaiah, how does it happen that not one of them ever conceived the like design in respect of the parallel place in S. Mark?

3. It naturally follows to ask, Why are we to suspect the mass of the MSS. of having experienced such wholesale depravation in respect of the text of S. Matthew in this place, while yet we recognize in them such a marked constancy to their own peculiar type — which is *not* the text of Isaiah?

4. Here may be seen the general fidelity of the ancient copyists. For whereas in S. Matthew it is invariably ὁ λαὸς οὗτος, yet in the copies of S. Mark it is invariably οὗτος ὁ λαὸς (except of course in Codd. **B** and D; copies of the Old Latin and the Vulgate; the Peshitto. But is it reasonable that the very copies which have been in this way accused of licentiousness in respect of S. Mark 7:6 should be permitted to dictate to us against the great heap of copies in respect of their exhibition of S. Matthew 15:8?

And yet, if the discrepancy between Codd. **B** and ℵ on the one side, and the great bulk of the copies on the other did not originate in the way insisted on by the critics, how is it to be accounted for? It is seldom practicable to institute such an inquiry, because there is so much unbounded licence, flagrant carelessness, arbitrary interpolations, omissions without number, that disfigure **B** and ℵ in every page. But the case is materially changed when so many of the oldest of the Fathers, and all the oldest versions seem to be at one with **B** and ℵ. Then favor me with undivided attention while I explain how the misapprehension of Griesbach, Tischendorf, Tregelles, and the rest, have arisen. About the MSS. and the versions these critics are sufficiently accurate. But they have fatally misapprehended the import of the Patristic evidence..

The established Septuagintal rendering of Isa. 29:13 *in the Apostolic age* proves to have been this: ἐγγίζει μοι ὁ λαὸς οὗτος τοῖς χείλεσιν αὐτῶν τιμῶσί με. The words ἐν τῷ στόματι αὐτῶν, καὶ ἐν were omitted. This is certain. Justin Martyr and Cyril of Alexandria in two places so quotes the passage. Procopius Gazaeus in his commentary on Origen's Hexapla of Isaiah says expressly that the six words in question were introduced into the text of the Septuagint by Aquila, Symmachus, and Theodotion. Accordingly, they are often observed to be absent from MSS. They are not found, for example in the Codex Alexandrinus.

But the asyndeton resulting from the suppression of these words was felt to be intolerable. In fact, without a colon point between οὗτος and τοῖς, the result is without meaning. When once the complementary words have been withdrawn, ἐγγίζει μοι at the beginning of the sentence is worse than superfluous; it fatally encumbers the sense. To drop those two words, after the example of the parallel place in S. Mark's Gospel, became thus an obvious proceeding. Accordingly the author of the so-called second Epistle of Clemens Romanus professing to quote the place in the prophet Isaiah exhibits it thus: ὁ λαὸς οὗτος τοῖς χείλεσί με τιμᾷ. Clemens Alexandrinus certainly does the same thing on at least two occasions. So does Chrysostom. So does Theodoret.

Thus two facts have emerged, which entirely change the aspect of the problem; (a) that the words ἐν τῷ στόματι αὐτῶν καὶ ἐν were anciently absent from the Septuagintal reading of Isaiah 29:13; (b) that the place of Isaiah was freely quoted by the ancients without the initial words ἐγγίζει μοι.

After this discovery will anyone be so perverse as to deny that on the contrary it must be Codexes B and ℵ, and not the great bulk of the MSS. which exhibit a text corrupted by the influence of the Septuagint reading of Isaiah 29:13? The precise extent to which the assimilating influence of the parallel place in S. Mark's Gospel may have been felt by the copyists I do not presume to determine. The essential point is that the omission from S. Matthew 15:8 of the words τῷ στόματι αὐτῶν, καὶ is certainly due in the first instance to the ascertained Septuagint omission of those very words in Isaiah 29:13.

But that the text of S. Mark 7:6 has exercised an assimilating influence on the quotation from Isaiah is demonstrable. For there can be no doubt that Isaiah's phrase (retained by S. Matthew) is ὁ λαὸς οὗτος, and that S. Mark's is οὗτος ὁ λαὸς. And yet when Clemens Romanus quotes Isaiah he begins with the same words as S. Mark, οὗτος ὁ λαὸς; and so twice does Theodoret.

The reader is now in a position to judge how much attention is due to Dr. Tregelles' dictum 'that this one passage may be relied upon' in support of the peculiar views he advocates — as well as to his confident claim that the fuller text which is found in ninety-nine MSS. out of a hundred 'must be regarded as an amplification borrowed from the Prophet.' It has been shown that in the ancient Greek text of the prophet the 'amplification' he speaks of did not exist — it was the abbreviated text which was found there. So that the very converse of the phenomenon he supposes has taken place. For freely accepting his hypothesis that we have here a process of assimilation, occasioned by the Septuagintal text of Isaiah, we differ from him only as to the direction in which that assimilation has manifested itself. He assumes that the bulk of the MSS. have been conformed to the generally received reading of Isaiah 29:13. But it has been shown that, on the contrary, it is the two oldest MSS. which have experienced assimilation. Their prototypes were depraved in this way at an exceedingly remote period.

To state this matter somewhat differently: In all the extant uncials but five, and in almost every known cursive copy of the Gospels, the words τῷ στόματι αὐτῶν, καὶ are found to belong to S. Matt. 15:8. How is the presence of those words to be accounted for? The reply is obvious. By the fact that they must have existed in the original autograph of S. Matthew. This is not the reply of Griesbach and his followers. They insist that beyond all doubt those words must have been imported into the Gospel from Isaiah 29:13. But I have shown that this is impossible, because at the time spoken of the words in question *were not in* the Greek text of the prophet. And this discovery exactly reverses the problem and brings out the directly opposite result. For now we discover that we have rather to inquire how is the absence of the words in question from those few MSS. out of the mass to be accounted for? The two oldest Codexes are convicted of exhibiting a text which has been corrupted by the influence of the oldest Septuagint reading of Isaiah 29:13.

I freely admit that it is in a high degree remarkable that five ancient versions, and all those early writers should all quote S. Matthew in this place from a faulty text. But this does not prove at how extremely remote a period the corruption must have begun. It probably dates from the first century. Especially does it seem to show how distrustful we should be of our oldest authorities, when, as here, they are plainly at variance with the whole torrent of manuscript authority. This is indeed no ordinary case. There are elements of distrust here, such as are not commonly encountered.

Matthew 5:44

An apt illustration may be found in our Lord's Sermon on the Mount (Matt. 5:44), which is in almost every MS. in existence as follows:

(1) ἀγαπᾶτε τοὺς ἐχθροὺς ὑμῶν,
(2) εὐλογεῖτε τοὺς καταρωμένους ὑμᾶς,
(3) καλῶς ποιέτε τοῖς μισοῦσιν ὑμᾶς,
(4) καὶ προσεύχεσθε ὑπὲρ τῶν ἐπηρεαζόντων ὑμᾶς,
(5) καὶ διωκόντων ὑμᾶς

I have numbered the clauses for convenience in studying this place.

On the other hand, it is not to be denied that there exists an appreciable body of evidence for exhibiting the passage in a shorter form. The fact that Origen reads the place six times in the following way:

ἀγαπᾶτε τοὺς ἐχθροὺς ὑμῶν,
καὶ προσεύχεσθε ὑπὲρ τῶν διωκόντων ὑμᾶς.

(which amounts to a rejection of the second, third and fourth clauses). Origen is supported in this by אּN, a few cursives, the Curetonian, the Lewis, several Old Latin MSS., and the Bohairic. This seems to critics of a certain school a circumstance fatal to the credit of those clauses. They are aware that Cyprian; Tertullian once; Theodoret once; Irenaeus; Eusebius, and Gregory of Nyssa exhibit the place in the same way. So does the author of the Dialogus contra Marcionitas, whom however I take to be Origen. Griesbach, on far slenderer evidence, was for obelizing all the three clauses. But Lachmann, Tregelles, Tischendorf and the Revisers reject them entirely. I am persuaded they are grievously mistaken, and that the Received Text represents what S. Matthew actually wrote. For it is the text of all the uncials but two, of all the cursives but six or seven, and this alone ought to be decisive. Also it is the reading of the Peshitto, the Harkleian and the Gothic, as well as of three copies of the Old Latin.

But let us inquire more closely for the evidence of the versions and Fathers on this subject, remembering that the dispute is nothing else but whether clauses 2, 3 and 4 are genuine Scripture. At the start we make the notable discovery that Origen, whose practice was relied on for retaining none but the first and fifth clauses, himself twice quotes the first clause in connection with the fourth clause.

Also Theodoret on two occasions connects clause 1 with what he evidently means for clause 2. And Tertullian once, if not twice, connects closely clauses 1 and 2; and once clauses 1, 2 and 5. From this it is plain that neither Origen nor Theodoret, least of all Tertullian, can be held to disallow the clauses in question. On the contrary, they recognize them, and this is a fatal circumstance to hostile evidence, effectively disposing of these men as witnesses against the clauses.

But in fact the Western Church yields unfaltering testimony also. Besides the three copies of the Old Latin which exhibit all five clauses, the Vulgate retains the first, third, fourth and fifth. Augustine quotes consecutively clauses 1, 3, 5; Ambrose quotes clauses 1, 3, 4, 5; again 1, 4, 5; Hilary clauses 1, 4 and 5, and again apparently 2, 4, 5; Lucifer, clauses 1, 2 3, apparently also 5; ps.-Epiphanius connects clauses 1, 3; also 1, 3, 5; and Pacian, clauses 5, 2.

As to the Greek Fathers, Chrysostom quotes the fourth clause five times; also consecutively clauses 1, 3; 1, 4; 2, 4; 4, 3; 5; 4, 5; 1, 2, 4; 1, 3, 4, 5, thus recognizing them all (iii. 167; iv. 619; v. 436; ii 340; v. 56; xii 654; ii 258; iii 341; iv 267; and xii 425).

Gregory Nyss. quotes connectedly clauses 3, 4, 5; Eusebius clauses 4, 5; 2, 4, 5; 1, 3, 4, 5. The Apostolic Constitutions (third century) quotes clauses 1, 3, 4, 5, after having quoted clause 2; also again clauses 2, 4, 1.

Clemens Alex. quotes clauses 1, 2, 4. Athenagoras quotes clauses 1, 2, 5. Theophilus quotes clauses 1, 4. Justin Martyr paraphrases clause 1, then connects it with clauses 2 and 4. Polycarp apparently connects clauses 4 and 5. The Didache quotes 2, 4, 5; and combines 1 and 3 (pp. 5, 6).

In the face of all this evidence, it is presumed no one will any more dispute the genuineness of the generally received reading in S. Matt. 5:44. A text so familiarly known in the age immediately after the Apostles could not have been shortened to clauses 1 and 5. By no possibility could the men of that age in referring to S. Matt. 5:44 have freely mentioned, *'blessing those who curse; doing good to those who hate; and praying for those who despitefully use.'* Since there are but two alternative readings of the passage — one longer, and one briefer. For every clear acknowledgment of a single disputed clause in the larger reading necessarily carries with it all the rest.

This result of 'comparative criticism' is therefore respectfully recommended to the notice of the learned. If it is not decisive of the point at issue to find such a torrent of very primitive testimony, and that at one with the bulk of the uncial and cursive MSS., then it is clear that there can be no Science of Textual Criticism. The Law of Evidence must be held to be inoperative in this subject-matter if the above testimony is rejected. Then nothing deserving of the name of 'proof' will ever be attainable in this department of investigation.

But if men admit that the ordinarily received text of S. Matt. 5:44 has been clearly established, then let the legitimate results of the foregoing discussion be loyally recognized The unique value of MSS. in declaring the exact text of Scripture — the conspicuous inadequacy of Patristic evidence by themselves — have been made apparent. And yet it has been shown that Patristic quotations are abundantly sufficient for their proper purpose, which is to enable us to decide between conflicting readings. One more indication has been obtained of the corruptness of the text which Origen employed — concerning which he is so strangely communicative — and of which B𝔑 are the chief surviving examples. Also here the probability has been strengthened that when these are the sole, or even the principal witnesses, for any particular reading, that reading will prove to be corrupt.

Mill was of the opinion — and of course his opinion finds favor with Griesbach, Tischendorf and the rest — that these three clauses have been imported from S. Luke 6:27, 28. But, besides the fact that this is mere unsupported conjecture, how does it come to pass that the order of the second and third clauses in S. Matthew is the reverse of the order in S. Luke? No, I believe there has been excision here; for I hold with Griesbach that it cannot have been the result of accident. [5]

It must be borne in mind that this is a question of both negative and positive: negative on the side of our opponents, with all the difficulties involved in establishing a negative conclusion as to the non-existence in S. Matthew's Gospel of clauses 2, 3, 5 — and positive for us in the establishment of those clauses as part of the genuine text in the passage which we are considering. If we can so establish the clauses, or indeed any one of them, then the case against us must fail. But unless we can establish all, we have not proved everything that we seek to demonstrate. Our first object is to make the adverse position untenable. Having done that, we fortify our own position. Therefore we have drawn attention to the fact that our authorities are summoned as witnesses to the early existence in each case of 'some of the clauses,' if they do not depose to all of them. We have with us the advantage of positive, as against their negative evidence. This advantage especially rules in such an instance as the present, because alien circumstances govern the quotation and regulate particularly the length of it. Such quotation is always liable to shortening, whether by leaving out intermediate clauses, or by sudden curtailment in the midst of the passage. Therefore, actual citation of separate clauses, being undesigned and fortuitous, is much more valuable than omission arising from whatever cause.

2. In answer to one who says that 'all four clauses are read by both texts,' (i.e. in both Matthew and Luke). But this one seems to be unaware of the present purpose of the existence of the fifth clause, or half clause, in S. Matthew. Yet the words, ὑπέρ ... τῶν διωκόντων ὑμᾶς are a very label, telling incontestibly the origin of many of the quotations. Sentences so distinguished with S. Matthew's label cannot have come from S. Luke's Gospel. The appearance of ὑπέρ — instead of the περί which ℵBLΞ exhibits in S. Luke — should be to our opponents a sign betraying the origin.

3. Nor again does the reviewer seem to have noticed the effects of the context in showing to which source a quotation is to be referred. It is a common custom for Fathers to quote verse 45 in S. Matthew, which is hardly conceivable if they had S. Luke 6:27, 28 before them, or even if they are quoting from memory. Other points in the context of greater or less importance are often found in the sentence or sentences preceding or following the words quoted, and are decisive of the reference. We give the references as we now know them below.

ON THE OMISSION OF SHORT CLAUSES

Especially we need to be on our guard against conniving at the ejection of short clauses consisting of twelve to fourteen letters. For this is commonly the length of a line in the earliest uncials. When such omissions leave the sense manifestly imperfect, no evil consequence can result. Critics then either take no notice of the circumstance, or simply remark in passing that the omission has been the result of accident. In this way οἱ πατέρες αὐτῶν is omitted by Cod. B in S. Luke 6:26, yet it is retained by all the Editors. And the strange reading of Cod. ℵ in S. John 6:55, where two lines are omitted, was corrected on the manuscript in the seventh century, and has met with no assent in modern times:

We show the omitted lines in brackets below:

ΗΓΑΡ
ΣΑΡΞΜΟΥΑΑΛΗΘΩΣ
[ΕΣΤΙΒΡΩΣΙΣΚΑΙ
ΤΟΑΙΜΑΜΟΥΑΛΗΘΩΣ]
ΕΣΤΙΠΟΣΙΣ

The ending of ΩΣ on the first and third lines explains how the copyist omitted lines 2 and 3 of the above.

But when, notwithstanding the omission of two or three words the sense of the sense of the context remains unimpaired, the clause being of independent signification, then great danger arises lest an attempt should be made to defraud the Church of a part of her inheritance through the officiousness of modern Criticism. In this way **καὶ οἱ σὺν αὐτῷ** is omitted from S. Luke 8:45 by Westcott/Hort, and they are included in brackets by Tregelles as if the words were of doubtful authority. And this is solely because some scribe omitted a line and was followed by **B**, a few cursives, the Sahidic, Curetonian, Lewis, and Jerusalem versions.

When the omission dates from an exceedingly remote period, having taken place in the second or third century, then the fate of such omitted words may be predicted with certainty. Their doom is sealed, inasmuch as every copy made from that defective original will reproduce the defects in its prototype. And if some of those copies have descended to our times, they will be quoted as if they were independent witnesses. Nor is this all. Let the taint be communicated to certain copies of the Old Latin, and we find ourselves confronted with very venerable foes, and thus formidable. And according to the recently approved method of editing the New Testament, the clause is allowed no quarter. Editors feel free to without hesitation declare the omitted words to be a spurious accretion to the Text. An instance of this can be seen in the following passage of S.Luke 12:39: *"If the master of the house had known in what hour his house the thief is coming."* etc. Here a clause has been omitted as seen within brackets:

ΟΚΛΕΠΤΗΣ
ΕΡΧΕΤΑΙ [ΕΓΡΗΓΟΡ
ΗΣΕΝΚΑΙ]ΟΥΚΑΝΑ
ΦΗΚΕΝ

The clause within brackets does not appear in Codd. ℵ and D. But the omission did not begin with ℵ. Two copies of the Old Latin are also without the words **ἐργηγόρησεν καί**, and they are also lacking in Cureton's Syriac. Tischendorf accordingly omits them. And yet, who does not see that such an amount of evidence as this is wholly insufficient to warrant the ejection of the clause as spurious? What is the 'Science' worth which cannot preserve a healthy limb to a body like this?

The instances of omission which have now been examined at some length must by no means be regarded as the only specimens of this class of corrupt passages. For one of the two most important omissions in the New Testament, see Appendix I; also see Appendix II. The fact is, omissions are much more common than additions, or transpositions, or substitutions. And this fact, that omissions are apparently so common, and that they at times are attested with seemingly strong evidence, cannot but confirm the general soundness of the contention that the preponderance of evidence must be consulted in each case. How, indeed, can it possibly be more true to the infirmities of copyists, to the verdict of evidence on the several passages, and to the origin of the New

Testament in the infancy of the Church, and that amidst associations that were not literary, to suppose that a terse production was first produced, and that afterwards it was amplified in a later age with a view to 'lucidity and completeness,' rather than that words and clauses and sentences were omitted in a small class of documents by careless, or ignorant, or prejudiced scribes?

CHAPTER 10 FOOTNOTES

Page 61: 'Dr. Dobbin has calculated 330 omissions in S. Matthew, 365 in S. Mark, 439 in S. Luke, 357 in S. John, 384 in the Acts, and 681 in the Epistles — 2,556 in all as far as Heb. 9:14, where it terminates (Dublin University Magazine, 1859, p. 620).

Page 61: ²Such as in Cod. D after S. Luke 6:4: 'On the same day He beheld a certain man working on the sabbath, and said unto him, Man, blessed are you if you know what you are doing; but if you do not know, you are cursed and a transgressor of the law' (Scrivener's translation, Intro., p. 8). So also a longer interpolation from the Curetonian after S. Matt. 20:28. These are condemned by internal evidence as well as external.

Page 63: ³καὶ ὁ ἐπὶ τὸν λίθον τοῦτον σθνθλασθήσεται ἐφ' ὃν δ' ἄν πέδ, λικμήσει αὐτόν.

Page 63: ⁴iv. 25 d, 343 d. — What proves these two quotations to be from S. Matt. 21:44, and not from S. Luke 20:18, is that they alike exhibit expressions which are peculiar to the earlier Gospel. The first is introduced by the formula οὐδέποτε ἀνέγνωτε (ver. 42; comp. Origen ii. 794 c), and both exhibit the expression ἐπὶ τὸν λίθον τοῦτον (ver. 44), not ἐπ' ἐκεῖνον τὸν λίθον. Vainly is it urged on the opposite side that πᾶς ὁ πεσών belongs to S. Luke — whereas καὶ ὁ πεσών is the phrase found in S. Matthew's Gospel. Chrysostom (vii. 672) writes πᾶς ὁ πίπτων while professing to quote from S. Matthew. And the author of Cureton's Syriac, who had this reading in his original does the same.

⁵ Theodoret once (iv. 946) gives the verse as Tischendorf gives it : but on two other occasions (i. 827 : ii. 399) the same Theodoret exhibits the second member of the sentence thus,—εὐλογεῖτε τοὺς διώκοντας ὑμᾶς (so pseud.-Athan. ii. 95), which shews how little stress is to be laid on such evidence as the first-named place furnishes.

Origen also (iv. 324 bis, 329 bis, 351) repeatedly gives the place as Tischendorf gives it—but on one occasion, which it will be observed is *fatal* to his evidence (i. 768), he gives the second member thus,—iv. 353 :

καὶ προσεύχεσθε ὑπὲρ τῶν ἐπηρεαζόντων ὑμᾶς.   ∴ 1. 4.

Next observe how Clemens Al. (605) handles the same place :—

ἀγαπᾶτε τοὺς ἐχθροὺς ὑμῶν, εὐλογεῖτε τοὺς καταρωμένους ὑμᾶς, καὶ προσεύχεσθε ὑπὲρ τῶν ἐπηρεαζόντων ὑμῖν, καὶ τὰ ὅμοια.   ∴ 1, 2, 4.—3, 5.

Justin M. (i. 40) quoting the same place from memory (and with exceeding licence), yet is observed to recognize in part *both* the clauses which labour under suspicion :   ∴ 1, 2, 4.—3, 5.

εὔχεσθε ὑπὲρ τῶν ἐχθρῶν ὑμῶν καὶ ἀγαπᾶτε τοὺς μισοῦντας ὑμᾶς, which roughly represents καὶ εὐλογεῖτε τοὺς καταρωμένους ὑμῖν καὶ εὔχεσθε ὑπὲρ τῶν ἐπηρεαζόντων ὑμᾶς.

The clause which hitherto lacks support is that which regards τοὺς μισοῦντας ὑμᾶς. But the required help is supplied by Irenaeus (i. 521), who (loosely enough) quotes the place thus,—

Diligite inimicos vestros, et orate pro eis, qui vos oderunt.
                        ∴ 1 (made up of 3, 4).—2, 5.

And yet more by the most venerable witness of all, Polycarp, who writes :— ad Philipp. c. 12 :—

Orate pro persequentibus et odientibus vos.   ∴ 4, 5.—1, 2, 3.

I have examined [Didaché] *Justin, Irenaeus, Eusebius, Hippolytus, Cyril Al., Greg. Naz., Basil, Athan., Didymus, Cyril Hier., Chrys., Greg. Nyss., Epiph., Theod., Clemens.*

And the following are the results :—

Didaché.   Εὐλογεῖτε τοὺς καταρωμένους ὑμῖν, καὶ προσεύχεσθε ὑπὲρ τῶν ἐχθρῶν ὑμῶν, νηστεύετε δὲ ὑπὲρ τῶν διωκόντων ὑμᾶς . . . ὑμεῖς δὲ ἀγαπᾶτε τοὺς μισοῦντας ὑμᾶς.   ∴ 2, 3, 4, 5.

Aphraates, Dem. ii.   The Latin Translation runs :—Diligite inimicos vestros, benedicite ei qui vobis maledicit, orate pro eis qui vos vexunt et persequuntur.

Eusebius ^{Prae} 654.   ∴ 2, 4, 5, omitting 1, 3.

Ps 699.   ∴ 4, 5, omitting 1, 2, 3.

Es 589.   ∴ 1, 3, 4, 5, omitting 2.

Clemens Al. 605.   ∴ 1, 2, 4, omitting 3, 5.

Greg. Nyss. iii. 379.   ∴ 3, 4, 5, omitting 1, 2.

Vulg.   Diligite inimicos vestros, benefacite his qui oderunt vos, et orate pro persequentibus et calumniantibus vos.   ∴ 1, 3, 5, 4, omitting 2.

Hilary, 297.   Benedicite qui vos persequuntur, et orate pro calumniantibus vos ac persequentibus vos.   ∴ 2, 4, 5, omitting the *first and third*.

Hilary, 303.   Diligite inimicos vestros, et orate pro calumniantibus vos ac persequentibus vos.   ∴ 1, 4, 5, omitting the *second and third*.   Cf. 128.

Cyprian, 79 (cf. 146).   Diligite inimicos vestros, et orate pro his qui vos persequuntur.   ∴ 1, 5, omitting 2, 3, 4.

Tertullian.   Diligite (enim) inimicos vestros, (inquit,) et orate pro maledicentibus vos—which apparently is meant for a quotation of 1, 2.

                                                              ∴ 1, 2, omitting 3, 4, 5.

Tertullian.   Diligite (enim) inimicos vestros, (inquit,) et maledicentibus benedicite, et orate pro persecutoribus vestris—which is a quotation of 1, 2, 5.

                                                              ∴ 1, 2, 5, omitting 3, 4.

Tertullian.   Diligere inimicos, et orare pro eis qui vos persequuntur.

                                                              ∴ 1, 5, omitting 2, 3, 4.

Tertullian.   Inimicos diligi, maledicentes benedici.   ∴ 1, 2, omitting 3, 4, 5.

Ambrose.   Diligite inimicos vestros benefacite iis qui oderunt vos : orate pro calumniantibus et persequentibus vos.   ∴ 1, 3, 4, 5, omitting 2.

Ambrose.   Diligite inimicos vestros, orate pro calumniantibus et persequentibus vos.   ∴ 1, 4, 5, omitting 2, 3.

Augustine.   Diligite inimicos vestros benefacite his qui vos oderunt : et orate pro eis qui vos persequuntur.   ∴ 1, 3, 5, omitting 2, 4.

'Benedicite qui vos persequuntur, et orate pro calumniantibus vos ac persequentibus vos.'   Hilary, 297.

Cyril Al. twice (i. 270 : ii. 807) quotes the place thus,—

          εὖ ποιεῖτε τοὺς ἐχθροὺς ὑμῶν,
          καὶ προσεύχεσθε ὑπὲρ τῶν ἐπηρεαζόντων ὑμᾶς.

Chrys. (iii. 355) says

          αὐτὸς γὰρ εἶπεν, εὔχεσθε ὑπέρ τῶν ἐχθρῶν [ὑμῶν],

and repeats the quotation at iii. 340 and xii. 453.

So Tertull. (Apol. c. 31), pro inimicis deum orare, et *persecutoribus* nostris bone precari.   ∴ 1, 5.

If the lost Greek of Irenaeus (i. 521) were recovered, we should probably find

          ἀγαπᾶτε τοὺς ἐχθροὺς ὑμῶν,
          καὶ προσεύχεσθε ὑπὲρ τῶν μισούντων ὑμᾶς:

and of Polycarp (ad Philipp. c. 12),

          προσεύχεσθε ὑπὲρ τῶν διωκόντων καὶ μισούντων ὑμᾶς.

¹ *Dialogus Adamantii* is not adducible within my limits, because 'it is in all probability the production of a later age.'   My number was eight.

CHAPTER 11

CAUSES OF CORRUPTION CHIEFLY INTENTIONAL
V. TRANSPOSITION—VI. SUBSTITUTION—VII. ADDITION

TRANSPOSITION

One of the most prolific sources of corrupt readings is Transposition, or the arbitrary inversion of the order of the sacred words. This generally occurs in the subordinate clauses of a sentence. The extent to which this prevails in codexes of the type of B℘CD passes belief. It is not merely the occasional writing of ταυτα παντα for παντα ταυτα, or ο λαος ουτος for ουτος ο λαος, to which allusion is now made. For if that were all, the phenomenon would admit of loyal explanation and excuse. But it is a systematic putting to wrong of the inspired words throughout the entire Codex — an operation which was evidently regarded in certain quarters as a lawful exercise of critical ingenuity. Perhaps it was even looked on as an elegant expedient to be adopted for 'improving' the style of the original without materially interfering with the sense.

Take for example S. Mark 1:5, where καὶ ἐαπτίζοντο πάντες is unreasonably turned into πάντες καὶ ἐβαπτιζοντο —whereby the meaning of the Evangelical record becomes changed, for πάντες is now made to agree with Ἱεροσολυμῖται, and the Evangelist is represented as making the very strong assertion that *all* the people of Jerusalem came to John the Baptist and were baptized. This appears only in BDLΔ.

And sometimes there are short clauses added, which I prefer to ascribe to the misplaced critical assiduity of ancient Critics. These obviously spurious accretions to the genuine text often bear traces of pious intelligence, and occasionally of considerable ability. I do not suppose that they 'crept in' from the margin, but that they were inserted by men who entirely failed to realize the wrongness of what they did, nor the mischievous consequences which might possibly ensue from their well-meant endeavors to improve the work of the Holy Ghost.

S. Mark 2:3 is changed by ℵBL from πρὸς αὐτόν παραλυτικὸν φέροντε 2 into φέροντες πρὸς αὐτὸν παραλυτικόν. A few words will explain to those not having carefully examined the effect of this *apparently* slight alteration. Our Lord was in a house at Capernaum with a thick crowd of people about Him. There was no room at the door. While He was teaching a company of people come to Him (ἔρχονται πρὸς αὐτόν), four of the party carrying a paralytic on a cot. When they arrive at the house, a few of the company, enough to represent the whole, force their way in and reach Him. But on looking back they see that the rest are unable to bring the paralytic near to Him. Then they all go out and uncover (dig through) the roof, take up the sick man, and the rest of the familiar story unfolds itself. Some officious scribe wished to remove all antiquity arising from the separation of παραλυτικόν from αἱρόμενον, which agrees with it, and transposed φέροντες to the verb that it is attached to, and in this way clumsily excluded the exquisite hint that in the ineffectual attempt to bring in the paralytic only *some* of the company reached our Lord's presence (those able to read between the lines will see the hint). Of course the scribe in question found followers in ℵBL.

It will be seen therefore that some cases of transposition are of a kind which is without excuse and inadmissible. Such transposition consists in drawing back a word which occurs further on, but it is thus introduced into a new context, and so gives a new sense. It seems to be assumed that since the words are all there, so long as they are preserved, their exact collocation is of no moment. Transpositions of that kind, to speak plainly, are important only as affording conclusive proof that such copies as BℵD preserve a text which is so obviously indefensible that the Codexes themselves are to be prized chiefly as beacon-lights preserved by a watchful Providence to warn every voyaging bark against making shipwreck on a shore already strewn with wrecks. In this regard note: B has 2,098 transpositions; ℵ has 2,299; D has 3,471.

Transposition may sometimes be as conveniently illustrated in English as in Greek. In Acts 2:45, 46 S. Luke relates that the first believers sold their goods *"and parted them to all men, as every man had need. And they, continuing daily,"* etc. For this Cod. D reads: "and they parted them daily to all men as every man had need. And they continued in the temple."

It is impossible to divine for what possible reason most of these transpositions were made. On countless occasions they do not in the least affect the sense. Often they cannot be idiomatically represented in English. Generally speaking they are of no manner of importance except as tokens of the licence which was claimed by disciples, as I suspect, of the Alexandrian school — or exercised unintentionally by careless or ignorant Western copyists. But occasions do arise when we cannot afford to allow the Scriptures to be so trifled with. An important change in the meaning of a sentence is sometimes effected by transposing its clauses. On one occasion the prophetic intention of the Speaker is obscured in consequence. Consider S. Luke 13:9, where under the figure of a barren fig-tree our Lord hints at what is to befall the Jewish people, because in the fourth year of His Ministry it remained unfruitful: *"Lo, these three years come I seeking fruit on this fig-tree, and find none; cut it down; why does it cumber the ground?"* The Vinedresser answered, *"Spare it for this year also, and if it bear fruit, well; but if not, next year you shall cut it down."* But on the strength of ℵBLT some recent Critics would have us read: "And if it bear fruit next year, well; but if not, you shall cut it down" — which clearly would add a year to the time of the probation of the Jewish race. The limit assigned in the genuine text is the fourth year. In the corrupt text of ℵBLT, two bad cursives, and the two chief Egyptian versions, this period becomes extended to the fifth year.

To reason about such transpositions of words at times soon degenerates into the veriest trifling. Sometimes, the order of the words is immaterial to the sense. Even when a different shade of meaning is the result of a different collocation, what will seem the better order to one man will not seem so to another. The best order of course is that which most accurately exhibits the Author's precise shade of meaning. But of this only the Author is a competent judge. As for our side, an appeal to actual evidence is obviously the only resource. For in no other way can we reasonably expect to ascertain what was the order of the words in the original document. And surely such an appeal can be attended with only one result; that is, the unconditional rejection of the peculiar and often varying order advocated by the very few Codexes; and a cordial acceptance of the order exhibited by all other documents.

Note two samples of my meaning. It has been questioned whether S. Luke (24:7) wrote, λέγων, ὅτι δεῖ τὸν υἱὸν τοῦ ἀνθρώπου παραδοθῆναι, as all the MSS. in the world have it, except four. And it is also so in all the versions and all the available Fathers so attest. There is evidence to support it from A.D. 150 on. But אBCL represent S. Luke as having written, **λέγων τὸν υἱὸν τοῦ ἀνθρώπου ὅτι δεῖ παραδοθῆναι** — and those four documents only. (the point which first strikes a scholar is that there is in this corrupt reading a familiar classicism which is alien to the style of the Gospels, and which may be a symptom of an attempt on the part of some early critic who was seeking to bring them into agreement with ancient Greek models.) But surely also it is even obvious that the correspondence of those four Codexes in such a particular as this must be the result of their having derived the reading from one and the same original. Contrariwise, the agreement of all other documents in a trifling detail like this can be only accounted for by presuming that they also have been all derived through various lines of descent from a single document — and *that* document is the original autograph of S. Luke. For there being such a great number and variety of them, there is a necessity that they have been derived through various lines of descent. Indeed, they must have the notes of number, variety, as well as continuity, and also of weight.

On countless occasions it is very difficult, perhaps impossible, to determine *apart from external evidence* which collocation of two or more words is the true one. The burden of proof rests evidently with innovators on Traditional use. It is at the same time obvious that if one sits down before the Gospel with the deliberate attempt to 'improve' the style of the Evangelists by transposing their words on an average of seven times to a page, as **B** does (א eight times a page; D twelve times) — it is easy to convict himself of folly long before he has reached the end of his task. So when the scribe of א in place of **ἐξουσίαν ἔδωκεν αὐτῷ καὶ κρίσιν ποιεῖν** (John 5:27) presents us with this: **καὶ κρίσιν ἔδωκεν αὐτῷ ἐξουσίαν ποιεῖν**, we do not hesitate to say that he has written *nonsense*. And when BD instead of **εἰσί τινες τῶν ὧδε ἑστηκότων** exhibit **εἰσί τινες ὧδε τῶν ἑστηκότων**, we cannot but conclude that the credit of those two MSS. must be lowered in the eyes of anyone who has an appreciation of the niceties of Greek scholarship.

This characteristic of the old uncials is now commended to the attention of students. For they will find in the folios of those documents plenty of instances for examination. Most of the cases of Transposition are petty enough, but some constitute blots not favorable to the general reputation of the copies on which they are found. They are so frequent that they must have propagated themselves. For it is in this secondary character rather than in any first intention that Transpositions, together with Omissions, Substitutions, and Additions, that have become the independent causes of corruption. Originally produced by other forces, they have acquired a power of extension in themselves.

It is hoped that the passages already quoted may be found sufficient to exhibit the character of the large class of instances in which the pure Text of the original Autographs has been corrupted by Transposition. That it has been so corrupted is proved by the evidence which is generally overpowering in each case. There has in a host of cases much intentional perversion, along with carelessness and ignorance of Greek that causes inveterate inaccuracy. This is characteristic especially of Western corruption as may be seen in Codex D and the Old Latin versions. The result has been found in constant slurs on the sacred pages, lessening the beauty of it, and often perverting its sense. This must be a source of sorrow to the keen scholar and reverent Christian.

VI. SUBSTITUTION

All the corruption in the sacred Text may be classed under these four heads: Omission, Transposition, Substitution and Addition. Because we have arranged this volume as it is, Scientific Method has been neglected. The result must be that passages are capable of being classed under more than one head. But logical exactness is of less practical value than a complete and suitable treatment of the corrupted passages that actually occur in the four Gospels.

Therefore, it seems needless to supply with a boring scrupulousness a disquisition on Substitution which has not forced itself into a place amongst Dean Burgon's papers, although it is found in a fragmentary plan of this part of the treatise. The class of Substitutions is a large one, if also are included under this head Modifications. For example, B has 935 substitutions and 1,132 modifications, totaling 2,067. ℵ has 1,114 substitutions and 1,265 modifications, totaling 2,379. Codex D has 2,121 substitutions and 1,772 modifications, totaling 3,893. It will be readily concluded that some substitutions are serious, some of less importance, and many trivial. Of the more important class, the reading of ἁμαρτήματος for κρίσεως in S. Mark 3:29 is a specimen. The substitution appears in ℵBLΔ and three cursives. It is true that D reads ἁμαρτίας, supported by the first corrector of C, and three of the Farrar group (13, 69, 346); and that the change adopted is supported by the Old Latin versions except f, the Vulgate, Bohairic, Armenian, Gothic, Lewis and Saxon. But the opposition favoring κρίσεως is made up of A, C in the first reading, and in the second correction; ΦΣ and eleven other uncials, the great bulk of the cursives, the Peshitto and Harkleian, and f. The internal evidence is also in favor of the Traditional Text, both as regards the usage of ἔνοχος, and the natural meaning given by κρίσεως. And ἁμαρτήματος has clearly crept in from verse 28.

Other instances of substitution may be found in the well-known S. Luke 23:45, where an impossible eclipse is foisted onto the Text by a false reading (See the full discussion elsewhere in this volume under *The Revision Revised*.) Substitutions in S. Matt. 11:27 (βούληται ἀποκαλύψαι); S. Matt. 27:34 (οἶνον for ὄξος); S. Mark 1:2 ('Isaiah' for the 'prophets,' discussed before in this section); S. John 1:18 (ὁ μονογένης Θεός for ὁ μονογένης Υἱός, (which makes Jesus a begotten god); S. Mark 7:31 (διὰ Σιδῶνος for καὶ Σιδῶνος). These instances will suffice to show that substitutions can seriously deprave the sacred Text. Many of these changes arose from various causes which are discussed in many other places of this volume.

For a prime example of the doctrinal importance of a gross substitution see the learned and totally unanswerable defense of the traditional reading of 1 Timothy 3:16 by Dean Burgon in an Appendix to The Traditional Text herein.

VII. ADDITION

The smallest of the four classes of corruption is that of Additions. B has 536 words added in the Gospels; ℵ has 839; and D has 2,213. And the reason for there being a lesser number of Additions is easily discoverable. While it is easy for scribes or those who deem themselves Critics to omit words and passages, or even to vary the order, or to use another word or form instead of the right one, it is plainly a matter of much difficulty to insert anything into the sacred Text without it be glaringly noticeable for its unfitness. Therefore, insertions, or additions, or interpolations naturally will be fewer than omissions. There is no difficulty in leaving out large numbers of the Sacred Words; but there is much difficulty in placing in their midst mere human words. For these are possessed with such a character and clothed in such a uniform as to betray themselves to any caring, keen observer as being of earthly origin.

A few examples will demonstrate this truth. It is remarkable that efforts at interpolation occur most copiously among the books of those who are least fitted to make them. This is especially true of the representatives of the Western school where Greek was less understood than in the East. For Greek acumen was imperfectly represented by Latin activity; and where translation into Latin and retranslation into Greek was called for, there appeared a prolific cause of corruption. A good example appears in Cod. D in S. Luke 6:4: "On the same day He beheld a cretain man working on the sabbath, and said to him, Man, blessed are you if you know what you do; but if you know not, you are cursed and a transgressor of the law" — a gross attempt to pad the sacred Text.

Another example appears in the Curetonian Syriac in S. Matt. 20:28: "But seek ye from little to become greater, and not from greater to become less. When you are invited to supper in a house, sit not down in the best place, lest some one come who is more honorable than you, and the lord of the supper say to you, Go down below; and you be ashamed in the presence of them that have sat down. But if you sit down in the lower place, and one who is inferior to you come in, the lord also of the supper will say to you, Come near, and come up, and sit down; and you will have greater honor in the presence of them that have sat down" — who does not see that there is no real ring of genuineness here?

Conspicuous beyond all things in the incident of the Centurion at Capernaum was his faith (S. Matt. 8:13). It occasioned wonder even in the Son of Man. Do we not gather from the significant statement that his representatives found the ill servant whole the fact that the Centurion — having no need of confirmation of his belief — did not go with them, but enjoyed the twofold blessedness of remaining with Christ, and of believing without seeing? But see the clearly apocryphal statement found in אCEMUX: "And the Centurion returning to his house in that same hour found the servant whole" — giving the lie that the Centurion did not believe until he had actually seen the recovered servant. This is also found in about fifty cursives. And it does not improve the matter to find that Eusebius, besides the Harkleian and the Ethiopic versions, recognize the same appendix. We find no one yet who advocates the adoption of this patent accretion to the inspired text, in spite of the MSS. that contain it. For its origin is not far to seek, it obviously being inserted in order to give a kind of finish to the story.

Another remarkable Addition may be found in S. Matt. 24:36, into which the words οὐδὲ ὁ Υἱός (*"neither the Son"*) have been transferred from S. Mark 13:32 in compliance with a wholly insufficient body of authorities.[1] Lachmann was the leader in this proceeding, and he has been followed by Tischendorf, Westcott/Hort and the Revisers. How inadequate is the evidence will be quickly noted in this array of authorities supporting it: א in the first reading, and as re-corrected in the seventh century; BD; five cursives; ten Old Latin copies, also the Aureus; some copies of the Vulgate; the Palestinian, Ethiopic, Armenian versions; Origen; Hilary; Cyril Alex.; Ambrose. But Irenaeus, Cyril and Chrysostom seem to quote from the received reading of S. Mark. Also supporting the Received Text are: the chief corrector of א; FS with thirteen other uncials; all of the cursives except the five; the Greek MSS. of Adamantius and Pierus mentioned by Jerome; the Vulgate, the Peshitto, Harkleian, Lewis, Bohairic and Sahidic versions; Jerome; Basil, who contrasts the text of S. Matthew with that of S. Mark; Didymus, who is also express in declaring that the three words in dispute are not found in S. Matthew; St. John Damascene; Apollonius

Philosophus; Euthymius Zigabenus; Paulinus; St. Ambrose; and Anastasius Sinaita. Theophylact, Hesychius Presb., Eusebius, Facundus Herm. and Athanasius quote the words as being from 'the Gospel,' without reference, and therefore may refer to S. Mark. Phoebadius, though quoted against the Addition by Tischendorf, is doubtful.

The reader will judge from the evidence which is genuine. But at least they cannot surely justify the assertion by the majority of the Revisers that the Addition is only opposed by 'many authorities, some ancient.'

An instance occurs in S. Mark 3:16 which illustrates the carelessness and tastelessness of the handful of authorities to which it pleases many Critics to attribute ruling authority. In S. Mark 3:14 it had been stated that our Lord *"ordained twelve* (καὶ ἐποίησε δώδεκα); but because אΒΔ and C (which was corrected in the ninth century with a MS. of the Ethiopic) reiterate these words two verses later, in verse 16, Tischendorf and Westcott/Hort assume that it was necessary to repeat those words again in verse 16, though it was only two verses before which had introduced them. But eighteen other uncials, including ΑΦΣ and the third hand of C; nearly all the cursives; the Old Latin, Vulgate, Peshitto, Lewis, Harkleian, Gothic, Armenian, and other MSS. of the Ethiopic omit them. It is plainly unnecessary to strengthen such strong evidence with researches in the pages of the Fathers.

Explanation has been already given how the introductions to the Lections, and other Liturgical formulae, have been added by insertion into the Text in various places. Thus ὁ Ἰησοῦς has often been inserted (and Dean Burgon opines that in some places of the Received Text they are an Addition). The three most important additions to the Received Text, according to Burgon: ἐν τῷ φανερῷ in S. Matt. 6:18, having crept in from verse 6 against the testimony of a large majority of both uncial and cursive MSS. — ἐν ᾗ ὁ υἱὸς τοῦ ἀνθρώπου ἔρχεται in S. Matt. 24:13, which also has a superior weight of authority against it, per Burgon — and ἵνα πληρωθῇ . . . ἔβαλον κλῆρον in S. Matt. 27:35, where the quotation must be taken for similar reasons to have been originally a gloss.

[The reader is again reminded that in this section especially Edward Miller has taken Dean Burgon's notes and has pieced them out with his own comments.]

CHAPTER 11 FOOTNOTES

Page 77: 'It is notorious that a few copies of the Old Latin and the Egyptian versions exhibit the same depravation. Cyril habitually employed an Evangelium which was disfigured in the same way. But are we out of such materials as these to set about reconstructing the text of Scripture?

CHAPTER 12

CAUSES OF CORRUPTION CHIEFLY INTENTIONAL
VIII. GLOSSES

Glosses, properly so called, though they enjoy a conspicuous place in every enumeration like the present, are probably by no means so numerous as is commonly supposed. Certain it is that not *every* unauthorized accretion to the text of Scripture can be identified as a gloss. But a gloss is only those explanatory words or clauses which have insinuated themselves into the text, and of which no more reasonable account can be rendered than that they were probably in the first instance proposed by some ancient Critic in the way of useful comment, or necessary explanation, or thought to be a reasonable limitation of the actual utterance of the Spirit. So I do not call the clause νεκρούς έγείρετε in S. Matt. 10:8 a gloss. It is a gratuitous and unwarrantable interpolation; it is nothing else but a clumsy encumbrance of the text.

Glosses, or *scholia*, or comments, or interpretations, are of various kinds. Generally they are confined to Additions or Substitutions, since of course we do not omit in order to explain; and transposition of words already placed in lucid order, as the sacred Text may be reasonably observed to be, would confuse rather than illustrate the meaning. A clause, added in Hebrew fashion, which may perhaps appear to modern taste to be hardly wanted, must not therefore be taken to be a gloss. Sometimes a 'various reading' is nothing else but a gratuitous gloss, the unauthorized substitution of a common for an uncommon word. This phenomenon is of frequent occurrence, but only in Codexes of a remarkably untrustworthy type like BℵCD.

1. The disciples on a certain occasion (S. Matt. 13:36) requested our Lord to *explain* to them (ΦΡΑΣΟΝ ήμῖν—"They said") the parable of the tares. Every known copy but two; all the Fathers who quote the place (Origen five times; Basil; J. Damascene); and all the versions support the traditional text. But because Bℵ have ΔΙΑΣΑΦΗΣΟΝ —"make clear to us" — which is also Origen's reading on one occasion -- Lachmann, Tregelles, Westcott/Hort and the Revisers (but not Tischendorf) assume that διασαφησον stood in the inspired autograph. So they thrust it into the text, yet it is nothing but a palpable gloss. I am wholly unable to discern any connection between the premises of these critics and their conclusions.

2. S. Mark employs an obscure expression (7:3) to denote the strenuous frequency of the Pharisees' ceremonial washings, πυγμῆ. But in ℵ it is exchanged, but in no other copy of the Gospels, for πυκνά, which last word is of course nothing but a sorry gloss. Yet Tischendorf degrades πυγμῆ and promotes πυκνά to honor. Happily he stands alone in his infatuation. It is strange that the most industrious of modern accumulators of evidence should have been aware that by such extravagances he marred his pretension to critical discernment! Origen and Epiphanius (the only Fathers who quote the place) both read πυγμῆ. It ought to be universally admitted that it is a mere waste of time that we should argue out a point like this.

A little suspected gloss is the expression *"daily* in S. Luke 9:23 (καθ' ήμέραν). Found in the Peshitto and in Cureton's Syriac, but only in some copies of the Harkleian; also in most copies of the Vulgate, but largely disallowed by copies in the Old Latin; found also in Ephraem Syrus, but clearly not recognized by Origen; found again in אBA and six other uncials, but not found in CDE and ten others — the expression referred to cannot plead for its retention in the text higher antiquity than can be pleaded for exclusion. Cyril (if in such a matter the Syriac translation of his commentary on S. Luke may be trusted) is clearly an authority for reading καθ ημεραν in S. Luke 9:23, but he then elsewhere twice quotes that verse in Greek without it. Timotheus of Antioch, of the fifth century, omits the phrase. Jerome, although he allowed *quotidie* to stand in the Vulgate, yet ignores the word when for his own purposes he quotes the place. All this is calculated to inspire grave distrust. On the other hand, καθ ημεραν enjoys the support of the two Egyptian, the Gothic, the Armenian, and the Ethiopic versions. And in the present state of our knowledge, this must be allowed to be a weighty piece of evidence in its favor. But the case assumes an entirely different aspect the instant it is discovered that out of the cursive copies only eight are found to contain καθ' ἡμέραν in S. Luke 9:23. How is it to be explained that nine manuscripts out of ten in existence should have failed to transmit such a remarkable message, if it had ever been really so committed to writing by S. Luke? Tischendorf says the omission is explained by the parallel places. This is utterly incredible, as no one ought to know better than he himself. We now scrutinize the problem more closely, to discover that the very *locus* of the phrase is a matter of uncertainty. Cyril once makes it part of S. Matt. 10:38; Chrysostom twice connects it with S. Matt. 16:24. Jerome evidently regarded the phrase as a curiosity, informing us that *juxta antiqua exemplaria* it was met with in S. Luke 14:27. All this is in a high degree unsatisfactory. We ourselves are familiar with the *antiqua exemplaria* referred to by the Critic, and we freely avow that we have learned to reckon them among the least reputable of our acquaintance. Are they not represented by those Evangelia, of which several copies are extant, that profess to have been 'transcribed from, and collated with, ancient copies in Jerusalem'? These uniformly exhibit καθ' ἡμέραν in S. Luke 9:23. But if the phrase is a gloss, it is obvious to inquire how is its existence in so many quarters to be accounted for?

Its origin is not far to seek. Chrysostom, after quoting our Lord's saying about taking up the cross and following Him, remarks that the words 'do not mean that we are actually to bear the wood on our shoulders, but to keep the prospect of death steadily before us, and like S. Paul to *die daily.*' In two other places already quoted from his writings, Chrysostom is observed similarly to connect the Saviour's mention of 'bearing the Cross' with the Apostle's words, *I die daily.* Ephraem Syrus and Jerome persistently connect the same two places together. Jerome even cites them in immediate succession. The inference is unavoidable. The phrase in S. Luke 9:23 must be a very ancient expository gloss, imported into the Gospel from 1 Cor. 15:31 — as Mill and Matthaei long since suggested.

Sincerely regretting the necessity of parting with an expression with which one has been so long familiar, we cannot allow the sentimental plea to weigh with us when the Truth of the Gospel is at stake. It is certain that but for Erasmus, we would not have known this regret — for it was he that introduced καθ' ἡμέραν into the Received Text. The MS. from which he printed is without the expression; and it is also not found in the Complutensian. It is certainly a spurious accretion to the inspired Text.

[The reader's attention is invited to this last paragraph. The learned Dean has been sneered at for a supposed sentimental and effeminate attachment to the Received Text. He was always ready to reject words and phrases which do not have adequate support. Yet he denied the validity of the evidence brought against many texts by the school of Westcott/Hort, and therefore he refused to follow them in their surrender of the passages — Edward Miller.]

MANY 'VARIOUS READINGS' ARE BUT INTERPRETATIONS

Many so-called 'various readings' are nothing else but very ancient interpretations, therefore are but fabricated readings. Their value may be estimated by the fact that almost every trace of them has long since disappeared. Such is the substitution of **φεύγει** for **ἀνεχώρησεν** in S. John 6:15 — which Tischendorf thrusts into the text on the sole authority of **א**, some Latin copies including the Vulgate, and Cureton's Syriac. Tregelles ignores its very existence. That our Lord's *"withdrawal"* to the mountain on that occasion was of the nature of retreat is obvious. So Chrysostom and Cyril remark that He *fled* to the mountain. And yet both Fathers, like Origen and Epiphanius before them, are found to have read **ἀνεχώρησεν**.

Almost as reasonably in the beginning of the same verse might Tischendorf (with **א**) have substituted **ἀναδεικνύναι** for **ἵνα ποιήσωσιν αὐτόν**, on the plea that Cyril says, **ζητεῖν αὐτὸν ἀναδεῖξαι καὶ βασιλέα**. We may on no account allow ourselves to be imposed on by such shallow pretences for tampering with the text of Scripture; else the Deposit will never be safe. A patent gloss (rather an interpretation) acquires no claim to be regarded as the genuine utterance of the Holy Spirit because it is merely found in two or three ancient documents. It is the little handful of documents which loses in reputation.

In this way we are sometimes presented with what in effect are new incidents. These are not unfrequently discovered to be introduced in defiance of the reason of the case — as where Simon Peter is represented in the Vulgate as *actually saying* to S. John, "Who is it concerning whom He speaks?" (S. John 13:24) Other copies of the Latin exhibit, "Ask Him who it is," etc. **אBC** would persuade us that S. Peter only required that the information should be furnished to him by S. John, "Say who it is of whom He speaks."

By the change of a single letter (in **אBX**) Mary Magdalene is made to say to the disciples, "I *have seen* the Lord' (S. John 20:18). But then the new does not altogether agree with the old. Accordingly D and others paraphrase the remainder of the sentence thus: "and she signified to them what He had said to her." How obvious it is to foresee that on such occasions the spirit of officiousness will never know when to stop! In the Vulgate and the Sahidic versions the sentence proceeds: "and He told these things to me.'

The Hebraism **μετὰ σάλπιγγος φωνῆς μεγάλης** (S. Matt. 24:31) presents an uncongenial ambiguity to Western readers, as our own incorrect A.V. sufficiently shows. Two methods of escape from the difficulty suggested themselves to the ancients: (a) Since *"a trumpet of great sound"* means nothing else but a 'loud trumpet,' and since this can be as well expressed by **σάλπιγγος μεγάλης**, the scribes at a very remote period are found to have omitted the word **φωνῆς**. The Peshitto and Lewis so deal with the text, interpreting rather than translating. Accordingly, **φωνῆς** is not found in **אLΔ** and five cursives. Eusebius, Cyril Jerus., Chrysostom, Theodoret, and even Cyprian are also without the word. (b) A less violent expedient was to interpolate **καὶ** before φωνῆς. This is accordingly the reading of the best Italic copies, of the Vulgate, and of D. So Hilary, Jerome, Severianus, Asterius, ps.-Caesarius, Damascene and at least eleven cursive copies read the place. There can be no doubt at all that the commonly received text is right — it is found in thirteen uncials with **B** at their head; in Cosmas, Hesychius, Theophylact. But the decisive consideration is that the great body of the cursives have faithfully retained the uncongenial Hebraism, accordingly implying the transmission of it all down the ages. It is well to note that the three 'old uncials' (for A and C are not available here) advocate three different readings; the two wrong readings being respectively countenanced by our two most ancient authorities, viz. the Peshitto and the Italic versions. Tischendorf, as usual blinded by his partiality for א, contends here for the mutilated teext, and Westcott/Hort are disposed to do the same.

Recent editors agree that we should read S John 18:14 ἀποθανεῖν instead of ἀπολέσθαι: "Now Caiaphas was he who counseled the Jews that it was expedient that one man should *die* (instead of *perish*) for the people." There is certainly a considerable amount of ancient testimony in favor of ἀποθανεῖν (die); for besides אBC, it is found in the Old Latin copies, the Egyptian, and the Peshitto versions, besides the Lewis MS, the Chronicon, Cyril, Nonnus and Chrysostom. Yet it is certain that S. John wrote ἀπολέσθαι in this place. The proper proof is the consentient voice of all the cursive copies, except for 19 of loose character. In real fact, ἀποθενεῖν is nothing else but a critical assimilation of S. John 18:14 to 11:50 — somewhat as *die* is retained in our A.V. by King James' translators, though they certainly had ἀπολέσθαι before them.

Many of these glosses are rank, patent and palpable. Such is the substitution of ὅς ἄν τόπος μὴ δέξηται ὑμᾶς (in S. Mark 6:11) by אBLΔ for ὅσοι ἄν μὴ δέξωνται ὑμᾶς — which latter is the reading of the Old Latin and Peshitto, as well as of the whole body of the uncials, except those four, and of the cursives alike. Evidently some Critic considered the words which follow "when you go out *thence*" to imply that place, not persons, should have gone before. Accordingly he substituted '*whatsoever place*' for '*whosoever*.'[1] Another has bequeathed to us in four uncial MSS. a lasting record of his rashness and incompetency — but since he left out the words μηδὲ ἀκούσωσιν ὑμῶν, which immediately follow, it is easy to see that the fabricator has betrayed himself. Therefore, I am astonished that so patent a fraud should have recommended itself to Tischendorf, Tregelles, Lachmann, Alford, and Westcott and Hort. But in fact it does not stand alone. From the same copies אBLΔ (with CD) we find the woe denounced in the same verse on the unbelieving city erased (αμην λεγω υμιν, ανεκτοτερον εσται Σοδομοις η Γομορροις εν ημερα κρισεως, η τη πολει εκεινη). Quite idle is it to pretend with Tischendorf that these words are an importation from the parallel place in S. Matthew. A memorable note of diversity has been set on the two places, which in *all* the cursive copies is religiously maintained, viz. Σοδόμοις ἤ Γομόρροις in S. Mark; γῆ Σοδόμων καί Γομόρρων in S. Matthew. It is simply incredible that this could have been done if the received text in this place had been spurious.

Mark 14:41 and John 9:22

The word ἀπέχ   S. Mark 14:41 has proved a stumbling-block. The most obvious explanation is probably the truest. After a brief pause, during which the Saviour has been content to survey in silence His sleeping disciples — or perhaps after telling them that they will have time and opportunity enough for sleep and rest when He shall have been taken from them — He announces the arrival of *"the hour,"* by exclaiming ἀπέχει (It is enough, or sufficient; that is, the time for repose is over). But the 'revisers' of the second century did not perceive that ἀπέχει is used impersonally here; they understood the word to mean 'is fully come.' Therefore, they supplied the supposed nominative, viz. τὸ τέλος. Other critics who rightly understood απεχει to signify sufficient still subjoined *finis*. The Old Latin and the Syriac versions must have been executed from Greek copies which read ἀπέχζει τὸ τέλος; this being proved by the renderings *adest finis; consummatus est finis* in two Old Latin copies, from which the change in D was obvious. Other Latins copies similarly add *finis* or *consummatio*. The Peshitto more fully give it *appropinquavit finis, et venit sufficit*. But it is a suggestive circumstance, and an interesting proof how largely the reading ἀπέχει τὸ τέλος must once have prevailed, that it is frequently met with in cursives copies of the Gospels to this hour. Happily it is an 'old reading' which finds no favor at the present day.

Another instance of an ancient gloss introduced to help the sense appears in a reading of S. John 9:22: ἵνα ἐάν τις αὐτὸν ὁμολογήσῃ Χριστόν. So all the MSS. but one, and so the Old Latin, and all the ancient versions except the Egyptian. D. alone adds εἶναι; but εἶναι must once have been a familiar gloss. For Jerome retains it in the Vulgate; and Cyril when he quotes the place exhibits τὸν Χριστὸν εἶναι. Not so Chrysostom and Gregory of Nyssa.

Amid the incidents immediately preceding our Saviour's Passion, hardly any more affecting or more exquisite is that of the anointing of His feet by Mary the sister of Lazarus, which received its unexpected interpretation from the lips of Christ Himself: *"Let her alone. She kept it against the day of My burial."* (S. John 12:7) — He assigns to her act a mysterious meaning of which the holy woman little dreamed. She had treasured up that precious unguent against the day when His dead limbs would require embalming. But lo, she sees Him reclining at supper in her sister's house, and yielding to a Divine impulse she brings forth her costly offering and bestows it on Him at once. She little knew; she could not have known; that it was the only anointing those sacred feet were ever to enjoy. In a desire, I suspect, to bring this incident into an impossible harmony with S. Mark 16:1, a scribe is found at some remote period to have improved upon our Lord's expression: "Let her alone in order that against the day of My embalming she may keep it." Such an exhibition of the Sacred Text is its own sufficient condemnation. What that critic exactly meant, I fail to discover; but surely he has spoiled what he did not understand. It is quite true that אBD with five other uncial MSS. and Nonnus, four errant cursives, and the Latin, Bohairic, Jerusalem, Armenian and Ethiopic versions so exhibit the place, this instead of commending the reading only proves damaging to the witnesses by which it is upheld. no reliance is to be placed even in such a combination of authorities. This is one of the places which the Fathers pass by almost in silence. However, Chrysostom, and evidently Cyril Alex., as well as Ammonius convey roughly a better sense by quoting the verse with ἐποίησε for τετήρηκεν. Antiochus is express. The correct and Received Text reading is supported by A and eleven other uncials, and all the cursives but four, together with the Peshitto, Harkleian, Lewis, Sahidic, and Gothic versions. Such evidence is greatly superior to the opposing body, having number, variety, weight, and internal evidence. Also, with reference to continuity and antiquity, it plainly preponderates. As to the three 'old uncials,' D is full of blunders in the context, even omitting the next verse — B and ℵ are also inaccurate hereabouts.³

In S. John 12:7, in accordance with what has just been said, we find that the copies which it has recently become the fashion to adore (Bℵ) read; ἄφες αὐτὴν ἵνα ... τηρήσῃ αὐτό instead of ἄφες αὐτὴν εἰς τὴν ἡμέραν τοῦ ἐνταφιασμοῦ μου τετήρηκεν αὐτό. This startling innovation — which destroys the sense of our Saviour's words, and furnishes a sorry substitute which no one is able to explain⁴—is accepted by recent Editors and some Critics. Yet it is clearly nothing else but a stupid correction of the text, introduced by some one who did not understand the intention of the Divine Speaker. Our Saviour here is revealing to us an exquisite circumstance, what had until now been a profound and tender secret; viz. that Mary, convinced by many a sad token that the day of His departure could not be very far distant, had some time before provided herself with this costly ointment, and had *kept it* by her — intending to reserve it against the dark day when it would be needed for the embalming of the lifeless body of her Lord. And now it is but a week until that event. She sees Him reclining in her sister's house at supper amid circumstances of mystery which fill her soul with awful anticipation. With love's true instinct she divines that this may prove to be her only opportunity. So she "*anticipates* to anoint" (προέλαβε μυρίσαι, S. Mark 14:8) His body;, and yielding to an overwhelming impulse, she bestows on Him all her costly offering at once! How does it happen that some professed critics have overlooked all this? Anyone who has really studied the subject ought to know from a mere survey of the evidence on which side the truth lies in respect of the text of this passage.

John 17:4

In His Eucharistic address to the eternal Father our Lord speaks thus: '*I have glorified Thee on the earth. I have perfected the work which Thou gavest Me to do*"(John 17:4). Two things are stated: first, that the result of His ministry had been the exhibition on earth of the Father's glory;⁵ next, that the work which the Father had given to the Son⁶ was at last finished.⁷ And that this is what S. John actually wrote is certain—not only because it is found in all the copies except twelve of suspicious character (headed by ℵBACL); but because it is vouched for by the Peshitto, the Latin, the Gothic and the Armenian versions; besides a whole chorus of the Fathers: Hippolytus; Didymus; Eusebius; Athanasius; Basil; Chrysostom; Cyril; ps.-Polycarp; the interpolator of Ignatius; the authors of the Apostolic Constitution; Cyprian; Ambrose; Hilary; Zeno; Cassian; Novatian; Augustine — and of course by internal evidence. But the asyndeton (characteristic of S. John) proving uncongenial to certain of old time, D inserted καί. A more popular device was to substitute the participle (τελειώσας) for ἐτελείωσα; whereby our Lord is made to say that He had glorified His Father's name 'by perfecting' or 'completing' — 'in that He had finished' the work which the Father had given Him to do. This damages the sense by limiting it. Indeed it introduces a new idea. It would be hard to find a more patent gloss. Yet it has been adopted as the genuine text by all the Editors and Critics. So general is the delusion in favor of any reading supported by the combined evidence of ℵBACL, that the Revisers here translate: "I glorified Thee on the earth, *having accomplished* the work which Thou has given Me to do" — giving the English reader not a hint that they have altered the text.

Another example: when some came with the message, '*Thy daughter is dead; why troublest thou the Master further?*" the Evangelist (S. Mark 5:36) relates that Jesus *"as soon as He heard (εὐθέως ἀκούσας)* what was being spoken said to the father, *"Fear not. Only believe."* But for this אBLΔ substitute "disregarding (παρακούσας) what was being spoken" — which is nothing else but a sorry gloss, disowned by every other copy, including ACD and all the versions. Yet this sorry gloss finds favor with Tischendorf, Tregelles, and the others.

In the same way in the earliest age the construction of S. Luke 1:66 became misapprehended. Some Western scribe evidently imagined that the popular saying about John the Baptist (τί ἄρα τὸ παιδίον τοῦτο ἔσται) extended further, and comprised the Evangelist's record (καὶ χεὶρ Κυρίου ἦν μετ αὐτοῦ). To support this strange view καὶ was altered into καὶ γάρ, and ἐστί was substituted for ἦν. It is thus that the place stands in the Verona copy of the Old Latin. In other quarters the verb was omitted altogether; and that is how D, Evan. 59 with the Vercelli (a) and two other copies of the Old Latin exhibit the place. Augustine read it indifferently; but he insists that the combined clauses represent the popular utterance concerning John the Baptist. Unhappily there survives a notable trace of the same misapprehension in אBCL which alone of MSS. read καὶ γάρ . . ἦν.[8] The consequence might have been anticipated. All recent Editors adopt this reading, which however is clearly inadmissible. The received text, witnessed to by the Peshitto, Harkleian and Armenian versions, is obviously correct. Accordingly A and all the uncials except those named above, together with the whole body of the cursives, so read the place. With fatal infelicity the Revisers exhibit "For indeed the hand of the Lord was with him." They clearly are to blame, for indeed the MS. evidence admits of no uncertainty. So far as I can discover no ancient Greek Father quotes the place.

It seems to have been anciently felt, in connection with the first miraculous draught of fish, that S. Luke's statement (S. Luke 5:7) that the boats were so full that 'they were sinking' required some qualification. Accordingly C inserts *'just* sinking;' D has it 'within a little;' while the Peshitto, the Lewis and the Vulgate (and many copies of the Old Latin) exhibit *ita ut pene.* These attempts to improve upon Scripture, and these paraphrases, indicate zeal for the truthfulness of the Evangelist; but they betray an utterly mistaken view of the critic's office. The truth is, βυθίζεσθαι, as the Bohairic translators perceived and as most of us are aware, means *"were beginning to sink."* There is no need of any further qualifying expression.

As an explanation of the introduction of the name of Pyrrhus into Acts 20:4 as the patronymic of 'Sopater of Beraea,' is this: A very early gloss invented by some critic of the primitive age made Πύρου (or Πύρρου) out of Βεροιαῖος which follows. The Latin form of this was Pyrus, or Pyrrhus, or Pirrus. In the Sahidic version he is called the 'son of Berus,' which confirms me in my conjecture. But indeed, if it was with some *Beraean* that the gloss originated — and what is more likely? — it becomes an interesting circumstance that the inhabitants of that part of Macedonia are known to have confused the *p* and *b* sounds. Consider that if S. Luke actually wrote Σώπατρος Πύρρου Βεροιαῖος, why at the present day should five copies out of six record nothing of that second word? It certainly is a very early gloss, for it appears in the Old Latin. Yet the Peshitto knows nothing of it, and the Harkleian rejects it from the text. Origen and the Bohairic recognize it, but not the Ethiopic nor Chrysostom.

CHAPTER 12 FOOTNOTES

Page 82: ¹The attentive student of the Gospels will recognize with interest how gracefully the third Evangelist (S. Luke 9:5) has overcome this difficulty.

Page 82: ²Augustine with his accustomed acuteness points out that S. Mark's narrative shows that after the words of *"Sleep on now, and take your rest,"* our Lord must have been silent for a brief space in order to allow His disciples a slight prolongation of the refreshment which his words had already permitted them to enjoy. Presently, He is heard to say, *'It is enough'* (that is, 'You have now slept and rested enough'); and adds, *"The hour has come. Behold, the Son of Man is betrayed into the hands of sinners."*

Page 84: ³E.G. verse 1: all the three officiously insert ὁ Ἰησοῦς, in order to prevent people from imagining that Lazarus raised Lazarus from the dead. In verse 4 D gives the gloss, ἀπὸ Καρυώτου for Ἰσκαρίωτης; in verse 13 D spells thus, ὡσσανά; besides constant inaccuracies, in which is followed by none. The Sinaiticus Codex omits nineteen words in the first thirty-two verses of the chapter, besides adding eight and making other alterations. B is far from being accurate.

Page 84: ⁴*"Let her alone, that she may keep it against the day of My burying"* (Alford). But how *could* she keep it after she had poured it all out? 'Allow her to have kept it against the day of My preparation unto burial'(McClellan) — but ἵνα τηρήσῃ could hardly mean that; and the day of His ἐνταφιασμός had not yet arrived.

Page 84: ⁵ Consider John 2:11 and 11:40; Luke 13:17; Heb. 1:3.

Page 84: ⁶Consider John 4:34 and 5:36.

Page 84: ⁷Consider John 19:30. And see Luke 22:37.

Page 85: ⁸Though the Bohairic, Gothic, Vulgate and Ethiopic versions are disfigured in the same way; and the Lewis reads 'is.'

CHAPTER 13

CAUSES OF CORRUPTION CHIEFLY INTENTIONAL
IX. CORRUPTION BY HERETICS

The corruptions of the Sacred Text which until now we have been considering, however diverse the causes from which they may have resulted, have yet all agreed in this, that they have all been of a lawful nature. That is, at no stage of the business has there been *mala fides* in any quarter. We may make allowance for carelessness, even for licentious transcription. And we may invent excuses for mistaken zeal and the officiousness of men which has occasioned them not to scruple to adopt conjectural emendations of the Text. It has been shown with sufficient clearness that the number of distinct causes to which various readings may be attributed is even extraordinary.

But after the alarmingly large assortment of textual perturbations already considered, there remains some which refuse to fall under any of the heads of classification already enumerated. These cannot be accounted for on any ordinary principle. These are so exceedingly numerous, so considerable, as a rule so very licentious, that they transgress all regulations; they usurp so persistently the office of truth and faithfulness. Some present gross interpolations; some apocryphal stories; more often there are systematic lacerations of the text, or transformations as from an 'angel of light.'

We are constrained to inquire, How can all this possibly have come about? Have there been persons who made it their business of set purpose to corrupt the sacred Deposit of Holy Scripture which has been entrusted to us for the perpetual illumination of all ages until the Lord should come? Again we must be reminded that in the earliest age of all the New Testament Scriptures were subjected to notoriously evil influences. In the age which immediately succeed the Apostolic age there were a host of heretical teachers, who finding their tenets refuted by the plain Word of God then bent themselves against the Word with all their power. From seeking to evacuate its teaching, it was but a single step to seeking to falsify its testimony. Profane literature has never been exposed to such hostility. The inestimable value of the New Testament entailed greater dangers, as well as secured superior safeguards. Is it not strange that in this later age some should try to discard those same superior safeguards.

Satan could not even wait for the grave to close over S. John.[1]. Already there were many who taught that Christ had not come in the flesh. Gnosticism was already in the world. S. Paul denounces it by name (1 Tim. 6:20,) and significantly condemns the wild fancies of its professors, their dangerous speculations, as well as their absurd figments. Thus he predicts and condemns their pestilential teaching in respect to meats and drinks and concerning matrimony. In his epistle to Timothy he relates that Hymeneus and Philetus taught that the Resurrection was past already. What wonder if a flood of impious teaching broke loose on the church[2] when the last of the Apostles had been gathered in, and another generation of men had arisen? For then the age of miracles had departed, and the loftiest boast which any could make was that they had known those who had seen and heard the Apostles of the Lord (Acts. 20:29; Rev. 2:6, 13, 15).

The *'grievous wolves'* whose assaults S. Paul saw as imminent, and against which he warned the heads of the Ephesian church (Acts 20:29) did not long *"spare the flock."* While S. John was yet alive, the Nicolaitans had developed their teaching at Ephesus, and in the neighboring church at Pergamos. Our risen Lord in glory announced to His servant John that in the latter city Satan had established his dwelling-place (Rev. 2:13). Even while these awful words were being spoken to S. John, the men were already born who would dare to lay their impious hands on the Gospel of Christ.

No sooner do we find ourselves out of the Apostolic line, and among the monuments of the primitive age, than we are made aware that the sacred text must have been exposed at that very early period to disturbing influences which cannot be explained on ordinary principles. Justin Martyr, Irenaeus, Origen, Clement of Alexandria — among the Fathers — some Old Latin MSS., the Bohairic and Sahidic, the Curetonian and Lewis among the versions; and of the copies, **B** and **א**; and above all coming later still, Cod. D — these venerable monuments of a primitive age more than occasionally present us with deformities which it is worse than useless to extenuate, quite impossible to overlook. There are found in these unauthorized appendixes, tasteless and stupid amplifications, plain perversions of the meaning of the Evangelists, wholly gratuitous assimilations of one Gospel to another, and the unprovoked omission of passages of profound interest and not infrequently of high doctrinal import. How shall we account for such phenomena as these? In one quarter we light on a systematic mutilation of the text so extraordinary that it is as if some one had amused himself by running his pen through every clause which was not absolutely necessary to the intelligibleness of what remained. In another quarter we encounter the thrusting in of fabulous stories and apocryphal sayings which disfigure as well as encumber the text. How will anyone explain this?

Let me dispose at once of an uneasy suspicion which is pretty sure to suggest itself to a person of intelligence after reading what has just been said. The question is: If the most primitive witnesses are indeed discovered to bear false witness to the text of Scripture, where are we to take ourselves for the Truth? And what security can we ever hope to have that any given exhibition of the text of Scripture is the true one? Are we then to be told that in this subject-matter that the stream instead of getting purer as we approach the fountain head, on the contrary grows more and more corrupt? *Answer*: Nothing of the sort! The direct reverse is the case. Our appeal is always made to antiquity; and it is nothing else but a truism to assert that the oldest reading is also the best. A very few words will make this matter clear, because a very few words will suffice to explain a circumstance already adverted to, one which it is necessary always to keep before the eyes of the reader. The characteristic note, the one distinguishing feature, of all the monstrous and palpable perversions of the text of Scripture now under consideration is this: that they are never vouched for by the oldest documents *generally*, but only by a few of them — two, or three, or more of the oldest documents being observed as a rule to yield conflicting testimony (which in this subject-matter is in fact contradictory). In this way the oldest witnesses nearly always refute one another, and indeed dispose of one another's evidence regarding perversions of Scripture, testifying thus that they are untrustworthy.

I say then that it is an adequate, as well as a singularly satisfactory explanation of the greater part of those gross depravations of Scripture which admit of no legitimate excuse, to attribute them (however remotely) to those licentious free-handlers of the text who are declared by their contemporaries to have corrupted the Gospel. These blasphemous productions must once have obtained a very wide circulation; indeed they will never lack for someone to uphold them. What with those who like Basilides and his followers invented a gospel of their own — what with those who with the Ebionites and the Valentinians interpolated and otherwise perverted one of the four Gospels until it suited their purpose — what with those who like Marcion shamefully maimed and mutilated the inspired text — there must have been a large mass of corruption festering in the church throughout the immediate post-Apostolic age. But even this is not all. There were those who like Tatian constructed Diatessarons, or attempts to weave the fourfold Gospels into one — 'Lives of Christ' so to speak. And productions of this class were multiplied to an extraordinary extent. They not only found their way into the remotest corners of the church, but established themselves there. And will anyone affect surprise if occasionally a curious scholar of those days was imposed on by the confident assurance that by no means were those many sources of light to be indiscriminately rejected, but that there must be some truth in what they advanced? In a singularly uncritical age, the seductive simplicity of one reading — the interesting fullness of another — the plausibility of a third — was quite sure to recommend its acceptance among those many eclectic rescensions which were constructed by long since forgotten Critics. And from these came forth the most depraved and worthless of our existing texts and versions. Emphatically condemned by ecclesiastical authority, and hopelessly outvoted by the universal voice of Christendom, buried under fifteen centuries, the corruptions I speak of survive at the present day chiefly through that little handful of copies which the school of Lachmann, Tischendorf, Tregelles, etc. look upon as oracular. And calamitous to relate, many scholars are refashioning the Evangelical text under the mistaken title of 'old readings.'

PRINCIPLE AIM OF HERETICAL CORRUPTERS IS TO DENY THAT JESUS CHRIST IS CO-EQUAL GOD IN THE TRINITY

Numerous as were the heresies of the first two or three centuries of the Christian era, they almost all agreed in this: That they involved *a denial of the eternal Godhead of the Son of Man*; they denied that He is essentially very and eternal God. This fundamental heresy found itself hopelessly confuted by the whole tenor of the Gospel. Nevertheless, it assailed the Gospel with restless ingenuity; and many are the traces alike of its impotence and its malice which have survived to our own times —[and are being revived in our times—Ed.]. It is a memorable circumstance that it is precisely those very texts which relate either to the eternal generation of the Son — to His incarnation — or to the circumstances of His nativity — which have suffered most severely, and which retain to this hour traces of having been in various ways tampered with. I do not say that Heretics were the only offenders here; the orthodox were much to blame also as the impugners of the Truth. But it was at least a pious motive that moved the orthodox to tamper with the Deposit. They did but imitate the example set them by the assailing party. It is indeed the consequence of extravagances in one direction which often beget excesses in the opposite quarter. Accordingly, the piety of the primitive age did not think it wrong to fortify the Truth by the insertion, suppression, or substitution of a few words in any place from which danger from heretics was apprehended. In this way many an unwarrantable 'reading' is to be explained. This is not simply that 'marginal glosses have frequently found their way into the text — that points to a wholly improbable account of the matter. Rather, expressions that seemed to countenance heretical notions, or at least which had been made a bad use of by evil men, were deliberately falsified.

The heretics who first systematically depraved the text of Scripture were Basilides (fl. 134); Valentinus (fl. 140); and Marcion (fl. 150) — three names which Origen is observed almost invariably to enumerate together. Basilides and Valentinus are even said to have written Gospels of their own. Such a statement is not to be severely pressed, but the general fact is established by the abundant notices which the writers against heresies have cited and left on record. All that is intended by such statements is that these old heretics retained, altered, transposed, just as much of the fourfold Gospel as they pleased. Further, they imported into the Gospels whatever additional matter they saw fit — not that they rejected the entire inspired text. In the case of Valentinus it has been contended that his principal followers, who also were his contemporaries, put forth a composition which they were pleased to style the 'Gospel of Truth'. It would be idle to dispute as to the limit of the rashness and impiety of the individual author of the heresy. Valentinus probably did not individually go to the same length as Basilides, who was evidently a grievous offender in respect to S. Paul's Epistles as well as of the four Gospels. There is much confirmation that the so-called Gospels of Basilides, and of Valentinus, showed a preference for one particular Gospel before the rest, and was adopted by certain schools of ancient heretics. So a strangely mutilated and depraved text of S. Matthew's Gospel is related to have found especial favor with the Ebionites, with whom the Corinthians were associated by Epiphanius — though Irenaeus seems to say that it was S. Mark's Gospel which was adopted by the heretical followers of Cerinthus. Marcion's deliberate choice of S. Luke's Gospel is well known. The Valentinians appropriated to themselves S. John. Heracleon, the most distinguished disciple of this school, is deliberately censured by Origen for having corrupted the text of the fourth Evangelist in many places. A considerable portion of his Commentary on S. John has been preserved to us; and it is a very strange production indeed!

Concerning Marcion, a far more conspicuous person, he has left a mark on the text of Scripture of which traces are distinctly recognizable at the present day. A great deal more is known about him than about any other individual of his school. Justin Martyr and Irenaeus wrote against him, besides Origen and Clement of Alexandria, Tertullian in the West, and Epiphanius in the East. These elaborately refuted the teaching of Marcion, and have given us large information as to his method of handling Scripture.[1]

Another writer of this remote time who must have exercised sensible influence on the text of Scripture was Ammonius of Alexandria. But beyond every other early writer of antiquity it is Tatian who appears to me to have caused the most alterations in the Sacred Text.

It is obviously no answer to anything that has gone before to insist that the Evangelium of Marcion, for instance — so far as it is recognizable by the notices of it given by Epiphanius — can very rarely indeed be shown to have resembled any extant MS. of the Gospels. Let it be even freely granted that many of the charges brought against it by Epiphanius with so much warmth collapse when closely examined and severely sifted. It is to be remembered that Marcion's Gospel was known to be heretical; it is one of the many creations of the Gnostic age — therefore it must have been universally execrated and abhorred by the faithful among men. Besides Marcion's lacerated text of S. Luke's Gospel, there was an Ebionite recension of S. Matthew. Also there was a Cerinthian exhibition of S. Mark and a Valentinian perversion of S. John. We are but insisting that the effect of so many corruptions of the Truth, industriously propagated within far less than 100 years of the date of the inspired Scriptures themselves, must have made itself sensibly felt. Add the notorious fact that in the second and third centuries after the beginning of the Christian era the text of the Gospels is found to have been grossly corrupted even in orthodox quarters. Traces of these gross corruptions are discoverable in certain circles to this present hour, and it seems impossible not to connect the two phenomena together. The wonder is that we are able to distinctly recognize any evidence whatever at the end of so many centuries.

The proneness of these early heretics severally to adopt one of the four Gospels for their own explains why there is no consistency observable in the corruptions they introduced into the text. It also explains the bringing into one Gospel things which rightly and clearly belong to another Gospel, as in S. Mark 3:14.

In this section I do not propose to explain any considerable number of the actual corruptions of the text. But in no other way is it possible to account for such systematic mutilations of Sacred Scripture as are found in Cod. **B** — such monstrous additions as are found in Cod. D — such gross perturbations as are continually met with in one or more, but never in all, of the earliest Codexes extant, as well as in the oldest versions and Fathers.

The plan of Tatian's Diatessaron will account for a great deal. He indulges in frigid glosses (as when about the wine at the feast of Cana he reads that the servants knew 'because they had drawn the water;') or tasteless and stupid amplifications, as in the going back of the Centurion to this house. I suspect that the much discussed Scriptural passage (*"Why do you ask Me about that which is good?"*) may be referred to some of these tamperers with the Divine Word.

These professors of Gnosticism held no consistent theory. The two leading problems on which they exercised their perverse ingenuity are found to have been (1) the origin of Matter; and, (2) the origin of Evil.

(1.) They taught that the world's artificer ('the Word) was Himself a creature of 'the Father.' Encountered on the threshold of the Gospel by the plain declaration that *'In the beginning was the Word; and the Word was with God; and the Word was God;"* — and presently, *"All things were made by Him;"*they were much exercised. The expedients to which they had recourse were certainly extraordinary. Valentinus said that 'Beginning' was the first thing which 'the Father' created; which He called 'Only begotten Son,' and also, 'Only begotten God' [See John 1:18 in the *New American Standard Version* where this heresy is still being propagated— Ed.] Valentinus contended that God created the Word and implanted in Him the germ of all things. That is, seminally whatever subsequently came into being was in Him. He said that 'the Word' was the entire essence of all the subsequent worlds (Aeons), to which he assigned forms. From which it is plain that according to Valentinus 'the Word' was distinct from 'the Son'; who was *not* the world's Creator. Yet he acknowledged both to be 'God;' but only, as we have seen already, using the term in an inferior sense.

Heracleon, commenting on S. John 1:3, insists that 'all things' can but signify this perishable world and the things in it — not essences of a loftier nature. Accordingly, after the words 'and without Him was not anything made,' he ventures to interpolate this clause: 'of the things that are in the world and in the creation.' True, the Evangelist had declared with unmistakable emphasis, *"and without Him was not even one thing made that was made "*—but instead of *"not even one thing,"* the Valentinian Gnostics appear to have written 'nothing;' and the concluding clause 'that was made,' Valentinus boldly severed from the context, making it the beginning of a fresh sentence. This was because he found that clause simply unmanageable. So with the Gnostics verse 4 is found to have begun thus, 'What was made in Him was life.'

Of the change of **οὐδὲ ἕν** into **οὐδέν** traces survive in many of the Fathers; but ℵ and D are the only uncial MSS. which are known to retain that corrupt reading. The uncouth sentence which follows (**ὃ γέγονεν ἐν αὐτῷ ζωὴ ἦν**), singular to relate, was generally tolerated, became established in some quarters, and meets us still at every step. It was evidently put forward so perseveringly by the Gnostics, with whom it was a kind of article of the faith, that the orthodox at last became too familiar with it. Though Epiphanius condemns it, he once employs it. Occurring first in a fragment of Valentinus; next in the Commentary of Heracleon; after that in the pages of Theodotus the Gnostic (A.D. 192); then in an exposure by Hippolytus of the tenets of the Naaseni (a subsection of the same school) — the baseness of its origin at least is undeniable. But inasmuch as the words may be made to bear a loyal interpretation, the heretical construction of S. John 1:3 was endured by the Church for full 200 years. Clemens Alex. is observed thrice to adopt it; Origen and Eusebius fall into it repeatedly [Clemens and Origen did not believe in the eternal Godhood of Jesus, but it is surprising to see Eusebius make this error — Ed]. It is found in Codd. ℵCD, apparently in Cod. A, where it fills one line exactly. Cyril comments largely on it. But as fresh heresies arose which the depraved text seemed to favor, the Church bestirred herself and remonstrated. It suited the Arians and the Macedonians, who insisted that the Holy Spirit was a creature. The former were refuted by Epiphanius, who points out that the sense is not complete until you have read the words **ὃ γέγονεν**. A fresh sentence (he says) begins at **ἐν αὐτῷ ζωὴ ἦν**. Chrysostom deals with the latter, saying, "Let us beware of putting the full stop at the words **οὐδὲ ἕν**, as do the heretics. In order to make out that the Spirit is a creature, they read **ὃ γέγονεν ἐν αὐτῷ ζωὴ ἦν**; by which means S. John's meaning becomes unintelligible."

But in the meantime Valentinus, whose example was followed by Theodotus and by at least two of the Gnostic sects against whom Hippolytus wrote, had gone further. The better to conceal S. John's purpose, the heresiarch falsified the inspired text. In place of *"What was made in Him was life"* Valentinus substituted 'What was made in Him *is* Life.' Origen had seen copies so depraved, and he judged the reading not altogether improbable. Clement even adopted it on a single occasion. It was the approved reading of the Old Latin versions, a memorable indication from which quarter the Old Latin derived their texts — which also explains why it is found in Cyprian, Hilary and Augustine; and why Ambrose has so elaborately 'vindicated' its sufficiency. It also appears in the Sahidic and in Cureton's Syriac. But it is not in the Peshitto nor the Vulgate, nor in the Bohairic. In the meantime the only Greek Codexes which retain this singular trace of the Gnostic period at the present day are Codexes ℵ and D.

MORE INSTANCES OF THE OPERATIONS OF HERETICS

The Good Shepherd in S. John 10:14, 15 says concerning Himself, *'I know My sheep, and am known of Mine, even as the Father knows ME and I know the Father."* By these words He hints at a mysterious knowledge as subsisting between Himself and those that are His. And yet it is worth observing that whereas He describes the knowledge which subsists between the Father and the Son in language which implies that it is strictly identical on either side — He is careful to distinguish between the knowledge which subsists between the creature and the Creator by slightly varying the expression. In this way He leaves it to be inferred that it is not, nor can it be, the same on either side. God knows us with a perfect knowledge. But our so-called knowledge of God is a thing different not only in degree,but in kind. This explains the peculiar form which the sentence assumes: γινώσκω τὰ ἐμὰ καὶ γινώσκομαι ὑπὸ τῶν ἐμῶν.[2] And this very delicate diversity of phrase has been faithfully retained all down the ages, being witnessed to at this hour by every MS. in existence except four, BℵDL. The Syriac also retains it, as does Macarius, Gregory Naz., Chrysostom, Cyril, Theodoret, Maximus of the Fathers. It is a point which really admits of no rational doubt; for does anyone suppose that if S. John had written 'Mine own know Me,' 996 MSS. out of 1,000 at the end of 1,800 years would exhibit, *"I am known of Mine"*?

But in fact it is discovered that these words of our Lord experienced depravation at the hands of the Manichaean heretics. Besides inverting the clauses (and so making it appear that such knowledge begins on the side of man) Manes (A.D. 261) obliterated the peculiarity above indicated. Quoting from his own fabricated Gospel, he acquaints us with the form in which these words were exhibited in that mischievous production; viz. γινώσκει με τὰ ἐμά, καὶ γινώσκω τὰ ἐμά. We learn this from Ephiphanius and from Basil. In a paper where he makes clear reference to the same heretical Gospel, Cyril insists that the order of knowledge must be the reverse of what the heretics pretended. But then it is found that certain of the orthodox contented themselves with merely reversing the clauses, and so restoring the true order of the spiritual process discussed — and so disregarding the exquisite refinement of expression which clearly distinguished between God's knowledge of us and our knowledge of Him. Copies must once have abounded which represented our Lord as saying, 'I know My own, and My own know Me, even as the Father knows Me, and I know the Father' — for it is the order of the Old Latin, Bohairic, Sahidic, Ethiopic, Lewis, Georgian, Slavonic, and Gothic versions. But is is not the order of the Peshitto, Harkleian and Armenian versions. But Eusebius, Nonnus, and even Basil so read the place. But no token of this clearly corrupt reading survives in any known copy of the Gospels, except ℵBDL. Will it be believed that nevertheless all the recent Editors of Scripture since Lachmann insist on obliterating this refinement of language, going back to the reading which the Church has long since deliberately rejected? This is to the manifest injury of the Deposit. Some will say that this is many words about a trifle. Yes, to deny God's truth is a very facile proceeding; its rehabilitation always requires many words. But I request that the reader again carefully note that the affinity between ℵBDL and the Latin copies which universally exhibit this disfigurement once again is revealed. And once again the true reading receives no notice from Westcott and Hort, and so also of the Revisers.

OTHER DOCTRINAL CORRUPTIONS

The question of matrimony was one of those on which the early heretics freely dogmatized. Saturninus (A.D. 120) and his followers taught that marriage was a production of Hell. We are not surprised after this to find that those places in the Gospel which bear on the relation between man and wife exhibit traces of perturbation. Not asserting that the heretics themselves depraved the text, I state two facts; (1) That whereas in the second century certain heretical tenets on the subject of marriage prevailed largely, and those who advocated, as well as those who opposed, such teaching relied chiefly on the Gospel for their proofs; and, (2) It is accordingly found that not only does the phenomenon of 'various readings' prevail in those places of the Gospel which bear most nearly on the disputed points, but these readings are exactly of that suspicious kind which would naturally result from a tampering with the text, by both the opponents and the upholders of marriage. Take three examples:

S. Matt. 19:29	S. Mark 10:29	S. Luke 18:29
η γυναικα	η γυναικα	η γυναικα
deleted by BD,	deleted by אBDΔ,	all allow it
a‚b‚c, Origen	a‚b‚c, etc.	

Chrysostom remarks, ὅταν δὲ λέγῃ ὅτι "πᾶς ὅστις ἀφῆκε γυναῖκα," οὐ τοῦτό φησιν, ὥστε ἁπλῶς διασπάσθαι τοὺς γάμους, κ.τ.λ. (vii. 636 E.).

Παραδειγματίσαι (in S. Matt. 1:19) is another of the expressions which have been disturbed by the same controversy. I suspect that Origen is the author of a certain uncritical note which Eusebius reproduces in his *quaestiones ad Stephanum* on the difference between δειγματίσαι and παραδειγματίσαι; and that with him originated the substitution of the uncompounded for the compounded verb in this place. Eusebius certainly read παραδειγματίσαι (Dem. 320), with all the uncials but two, BZ; all the cursives but one. Will it yet be believed that Lachmann, Tregelles, Tischendorf, Alford, Westcott/Hort are prepared to reconstruct the text of S. Matthew's Gospel on such slender evidence?

It seems so like trifling with the reader's patience to invite attention to an elaborate discussion of most of the changes introduced into the text by Tischendorf and his colleagues, causing me to pass over many hundreds of instances where I am nevertheless perfectly well aware of my own strength and of my opponents' weakness. Such discussions in fact become unbearable when the points of dispute are confessedly trivial. No one, however, will deny that when three consecutive words of our Lord are challenged they are worth the time to contend for them. These Critics invite us to believe that our Lord did not utter the words in the following sentence from S. Luke 22:67, 68 which we have capitalized: *"If I tell you, you will not believe; and if I ask you, you will not answer ME, NOR LET ME GO."* Note carefully the grounds they have for deleting these words: they are missing only in אBLT, and in their ally the Bohairic version. Yet these words are in AD and 13 other uncials, and in every known cursive copy, as well as in all the Latin and in all the Syriac copies. Are we in spite of this torrent of overwhelming evidence to be assured that the words are to be regarded as spurious? Then note this: the heretic Marcion left out those words, and seven more words: "And I ask you... Me, nor let Me go" — and after noting this correspondence between the heretic and אBLT, will anyone doubt that the words are genuine?

CHAPTER 13 FOOTNOTES

Page 87: ¹ψευδωνύμου γνώσεως (1 Tim. 6:20).

Page 90: ²Celsus having objected that believers had again and again falsified the text of the Gospel, refashioning it in order to meet the objects of assailants, Origen replies: Μεταχαράξαντας δέ τό εὐγγέλιον ἄλλους οὐκ οἶδα, ἤ τοὺς ἀπὸ Μαρκίωνος, καὶ τοὺς ἀπὸ Οὐαλεντίνου, οἶμαι δὲ καὶ τοὺς ἀπὸ Λουκάνου. τοῦτο δὲ λεγόμενον οὐ τοῦ λόγου ἐστὶν ἔγκλημα, ἀλλὰ τῶν τολμησάντων ῥᾳδιουργῆσαι τὰ εὐαγγέλια (Opp. 1.411 B.)

Page 93: ³Consider 1 John 2:3, 4; and read Basil ii. 188 b, c. (where Basil proceeds exquisitely to show that man's 'knowledge' of God consists in his keeping of God's Commandments). Consider also Gal. 4:9.

CHAPTER 14

CAUSES OF CORRUPTION CHIEFLY INTENTIONAL
X. CORRUPTION BY THE ORTHODOX

Another cause why the Text of the Gospels underwent serious depravation in ver early times was mistaken solicitude on the part of the ancient orthodox for the faith. These persons, like some modern conservatives, and like Beza, did not think it at all wrong to tamper with the inspired Text. If any expression seemed to them to have a dangerous tendency, they altered it, or transplanted it, or removed it completely from the sacred page. About the uncritical nature of what they did, they entertained no suspicion. They evidently did not trouble themselves at all about the immorality of their proceedings. On the contrary, the piety of the motive seems to have been held to constitute a sufficient excuse for any amount of licence. The copies which had undergone this process of castigation were even styled 'corrected,' — and doubtless they were popularly looked upon as 'the correct copies' [like our 'critical texts' and 'new translations'] An illustration of this is afforded by a circumstance mentioned by Epiphanius: he states (2:36) that the orthodox, out of jealousy for the Lord's Divinity, eliminated from S. Luke 19:41 the record that the Saviour wept. We will not pause to inquire what this statement is worth, but when the same Father adds: "In the uncorrected copies is found *'He wept'*"Epiphanius is instructive. Being perfectly well aware that the expression is genuine, he goes on to state that 'Iranaeus quoted it in his work against heresies, when he had to confute the error of the Docetae.' Nevertheless, Epiphanius adds, 'the orthodox through fear erased the record.'

So then the process of 'correction' was a critical process conducted on utterly erroneous principles by men who knew nothing whatever about Textual Criticism. Such recensions of the Text proved simply fatal to the Deposit in some cases. To 'correct' was in this and such like cases simply to 'corrupt.'

Codexes B℧D may be regarded as specimens of Codexes which have been once and again passed through the hands of such a corrector. S. Luke 2:40 records concerning the infant Saviour, that *'the child grew, and waxed strong in spirit.'* By repeating the same expression which already had been applied to the childhood of John the Baptist (1:80),it was clearly the design of the Author of Scripture to teach that the Word *'made flesh'* submitted to the same laws of growth and increase as every other man. The body grew; the spiritual part waxed strong. This statement was nevertheless laid hold of by the enemies of Christianity, saying, 'How can it be pretended that He was perfect God, of whom it is related in respect of His spirit that He waxed strong?' The consequence might have been foreseen. Certain of the orthodox were ill-advised enough to erase the word **πνεύματι** (spirit) from the copies of Luke 2:40. And, lo, at the end of 1,500 years four 'corrected' copies, two versions, one Greek Father, survive to witness to the ancient fraud. And because it is ℵBDL, Origen, and the Latin, the Egyptian, and the Lewis versions, which are without the word **πνεύματι** Lachmann, Tregelles, Tischendorf, and the Revisers jump to the conclusion that it is a spurious accretion to the Text. They ought to reverse their proceeding, and to recognize in the evidence that this is one more indication of the untrustworthiness of certain witnesses. How can it be supposed that this word **πνεύματι** ever obtained its footing in the Gospel? We are assured by them that it was imported from S. Luke 1:80. We answer, How does the phrase **ἐκραταιοῦτο πνεύματι** in 1:80 explain that **πνεύματι** now can be found in every known copy of the Gospels except four, if in these 996 places out of a thousand it is an interpolation? Is it credible that all the remaining uncials, and every known cursive copy, besides all the lectionaries, should have been corrupted in this way? Is it credible to suppose that the truth should survive exclusively at this time only in the four uncials, **Bℵ** from the fourth century, D from the sixth, and L from the eighth?

When then, and where did this work of depravation take place? It must have been before the sixth century, because Leontius of Cyprus quotes it three times and discusses the expression at length; and before the fifth century, because Cod. A., Cyril,[1] Theodoret, and ps. Caesarius recognize the word — before the fourth, because Epiphanius, Theodore of Mopsuestia, and the Gothic version have it; before the third, also, yea, before nearly all of the second century, because it is found in the Peshitto. What is more plain than that we have before us one other instance of injudicious zeal of the orthodox; and one more sample of the infelicity of modern Critics?

Theodotus and his followers fastened on the first part of S. John 8:40, when they pretended to show from Scripture that Christ is mere Man. I am persuaded that the reading 'of My Father' — with which Origen, Epiphanius, Athanasius, Chrysostom, Cyril Alex., and Theodoret[2] prove to have been acquainted — was substituted by some of the orthodox in this place, with the pious intention of providing a remedy for the heretical teaching of their opponents. At the present day only six cursive copies are known to retain this trace of a corruption of Scripture which must date from the second century.

It will be remembered that S. John in his grand preface does not rise to the full height of his sublime argument until he reaches the eighteenth verse. In verse 14 he had said that *'The Word was made flesh,"*etc.; a statement which Valentinus was willing to admit. But the heretic and his followers denied that the Word is also the Son of God. As if to bar the door against this pretence, S. John in verse 18 announces that *'the only begotten Son, who is in the bosom of the Father, He has declared Him."* So he establishes the identity of the Word and the Only begotten Son. What else could the Valentinians do with so plain a statement, but to seek to deprave it? Accordingly, the very first time John 1:18 is quoted by any of the ancients, it is accompanied by the statement that the Valentinians appeal to the words 'the only begotten GOD who is in the bosom of the Father' — seeking to prove that the only begotten is 'the Beginning,' and is 'GOD'. They say that inasmuch as the Father willed to become known to the worlds, the Spirit of Gnosis produced the 'only begotten' 'Gnosis,' and therefore gave birth to 'Gnosis,' that is to 'the Son' so that by 'the Son' 'the Father' might be known. Then they say that while 'the only begotten Son' abode 'in the bosom of the Father,' He caused that there on earth should be seen one 'as the only begotten Son' (alluding to His being made flesh in verse 14).

But note that the author of Excerpta Theodoti (also a second century production) reads S. John 1:18 as we do.

These strange details are derived from documents which carry us back to the first half of the second century; there is no other way to explain and account for the text in S. John 1:18 being depraved. It is plain and easy to determine that in the transmission of this verse of Scripture there has been extraordinary perturbations. Irenaeus writes **μονογενής υἱός** once; **μονογενής**

Θεός once; μονογενής υἱός Θεοῦ once. Clemens Alex. writes μονογενής υἱός Θεός μόνος, which must be very nearly the reading of the Codex from which the text of the Vercelli Copy of the Old Latin was derived. Eusebius four times writes μονογενή υἱός, but twice μονογενής Θεός; and on one occasion he gives his reader the choice of either expression, 'explaining' how both must stand. Gregory Nyss. and Basil, though they recognize the usual reading of the place, are evidently vastly more familiar with the reading μονογενή Θεός; for Basil adopts the expression three times, and Gregory nearly thirty three times as often. This was also the reading of Cyril Alex, whose usual phrase however is ὁ μονογενής Θεός λόγος. Cyril of Jerusalem seems to have read ὁ μονογενής μόνος.

["I have retained this valuable and suggestive passage in the form in which the Dean left it. It evidently has not the perfection that attends some of his papers, and would have been amplified and improved if his life had been spared. More passages than he notices, though limited to the ante-Chrysostom period, are referred to in *The Traditional Text* [elsewhere in this volume—Ed.].

The most important part of the Dean's paper is found in his account of the origin of the expression. This inference is strongly confirmed by the employment of it in the Arian controversy. Arius reads Θεός (*ap*. Epiph. 73—Tischendorf), while his opponents read υἱός. So Faustinus seven times, and Victorinus Afer ten times in reply to the Arian Candidus. Also Athanasius and Hilary of Poictiers four times each, and Ambrose eight. It is curious that with this history admirers of B and א should extol their reading over the Traditional reading on the score of orthodoxy. Heresy had and still retains associations which cannot be ignored. In this instance some of the orthodox weakly played into the hands of heretics. None may read Holy Scripture just as the idea strikes them.

1 Corinthians 15:7

All are familiar with the text of 1 Cor. 15:47: *'The first man was out of earth, earthy. The second Man was the Lord of Heaven.* "That this place was so read in the first age is certain, for so it stands in the Syriac. These early heretics of whom S. John charged with denying that *"Jesus Christ had come in the flesh"* (2 John 7),[4] and who are known to have freely *taken away from the words"* of Scripture, are found to have been busy here. If they argued that *"the second" Man"* was indeed *"the Lord from Heaven,"* then they said, how can it be pretended that Christ took upon Himself flesh? And to bring out this contention of theirs more plainly, they did not hesitate to remove as superfluous the word 'man' in the second clause of the sentence. This resulted in a text saying: 'The first man was of the earth, earthy; the second Lord from Heaven.'[5] It was this way that Marcion (A.D. 130) and his followers read the place. But in this subject-matter extravagance in one direction is ever observed to beget extravagance in another. So I suspect that it was in order to counteract the ejection by the heretics of 'Man' in the second clause of verse 47 that, early in the second century, the orthodox retained ἄνθρωπος, but then judged it expedient to leave out the expression ὁ Κύριος (the Lord) — which had been so unfairly pressed against them. This left them contented to read, 'the second Man was from Heaven.' Truly this was a calamitous change; for first, the text mained in this way gave countenance to another form of mischief; and next it necessitated a further change in 1 Cor. 15:47.

1. It furnished a pretext to those heretics who maintained that Christ was 'Man' *before* He came into the World. This heresy came to a head in the persons

of Apolinarius and Photinus. Greg. Naz. and Epiphanius contending with them
are observed to argue with disadvantage from the mutilated (shortened) text.
Tertullian and Cyprian knew no other reading but 'second Man from Heaven'—
which is in fact the way this place stands in the Old Latin. And so from the second
century downwards two readings (for the Marcionite text was speedily forgotten)
became current in the Church: (1) the inspired language of the Apostle, which is
retained in all the known copies *except nine.* It is vouched for by Basil,
Chrysostom, Theodotus, Eutherius, Theodorus Mops., Damascene, Petrus
Siculus, and Theophylact. But (2) the maimed text ('the second man from
Heaven') is only known to survive in ℵ*BCD*EFG and two cursive copies.
Origen, and long after him, Cyril employed *both* readings.

II. But then, as all must see, such a maimed exhibition of the text was
intolerable. The balance of the sentence had been destroyed. S. Paul had set
against *the first man the second Man.* And he had set against *from the earth —
from Heaven;* and against χοϊκός (earthy) ὁ Κύριος (the Lord). If 'the
Lord' is removed, then some substitute for it must be invented as a counterpoise
to 'earthy.' Taking a hint from verse 48, someone suggested ἐπουράνιος; and
this gloss so effectually recommended itself to Western Christendom that it
established itself in the Vulgate (after having been adopted by Ambrose,
Jerome, and later by Augustine). So then, a *third* rival reading enters the field;
but because it has nearly disappeared from Greek MSS. it no longer finds an
advocate. It should be noted that Athanasius lends his countenance to *all three* of
the readings.

But now let me ask: Will anyone be disposed, after a careful study, to accept
the verdict of Tischendorf, Tregelles and the rest, who are bringing the Church
back to the maimed text, the history of which I have explained. Note that the one
question is this: Shall "the Lord" be retained in the second clause, or not? But
there it stood within thirty years of S. John's death; and there it still stands 18
centuries later in every extant copy (including AKLP) except nine. It has been
excellently witnessed to all down the ages; by Origen, Hippolytus, Athanasias,
Basil, Chrysostoim, Cyril, Theodotus, Eutherius, Theodore Mops., Damascene
and others. On what principle would you now reject it? It is vain to argue with
those critics who assume that any reading found in ℵBCDEFG must be genuine.
Yet the most robust faith ought to be effectually shaken by the discovery that four,
if not five (ℵACFG) of these same MSS. by reading 'we shall all sleep; but we
shall not all be changed,' in this same chapter, verse 51, thereby contradicting S.
Paul's solemn announcement that we *shall all* be changed. And a sixth of those
nine MSS (D) stands alone in substituting 'we shall all rise; but we   shall not all
be changed.' Then in this very verse C is for introducing *Adam* into the first
clause of the sentence; and FG for subjoining ὁ οὐράνιος. When will men
believe that guides like these are to be regarded with habitual distrust? These here
must   be listened to with the greatest caution; to be followed for their own sakes,
never!

I have been the fuller on this place because it affords an instructive example of
what has occasionally happened to the words of Scripture. Very seldom indeed
are we able to handle a text in this way. Only when the heretics assailed did the
orthodox defend — and by this a record was preserved of how the text was read
by an ancient Father. The attentive reader will note (a) that all the changes which
we have been considering belong to the earliest age of all; and (b) that the corrupt
reading is retained by ℵBC and their following; and that the genuine text is as
usual in the great bulk of the cursive copies; (c) that the first mention of the text is

found in the writings of an early heretic; (d) that the orthodox introduced a change in the interests, as they fancied, of truth, but from utter misapprehension of the nature and authority of the Word of God; and (3) that under the Divine Providence that spurious change was so effectually thrown out, that decisive witness is found on the other side.

John 3:13

Closely allied to the foregoing, and constantly referred to in connection with it by those Fathers who undertook to refute the heresy of Apolinarius, is our Lord's declaration to Nicodemus: *"No one has gone up into Heaven, but He that came down from Heaven, even the Son of man, who is in Heaven."* Christ came down from Heaven when He became incarnate; and having become incarnate He is said to have *"ascended up to Heaven,* and *"to be in Heaven"* because *'the Son of Man"* who was in Heaven before, by virtue of the hypostatical union was thenceforward evermore *"in Heaven."* But the language of S. John was taken by those heretics who systematically maimed and misinterpreted that which belonged to the human nature of Christ. Relying on the present place, Apolinarius is found to have read it without the final clause (*"who is in Heaven"*). And certain of the orthodox (Greg. Naz., Greg. Nyssa, Epiphanius) while contending with Apolinarius were not unwilling to argue from the text so mutilated. Origen and the author of the Dialogus once, Eusebius twice, Cyril nineteen times, also leave off the words 'even the Son of Man' — from which it is insecurely gathered that those Fathers disallowed the clause which follows. On the other hand thirty-eight Fathers and ten versions maintain the genuineness of the words ὁ ὢν ἐν τῷ οὐρανῷ (*"who is in Heaven"*). It is found in every MSS in the world except five uncials of bad character (אBLT) and one cursive (33). They are recognized by *all* the Latin and *all* the Syriac versions; the Coptic; the Ethiopic; the Georgian; and the Armenian versions. They are recognized, quoted, or insisted on by Origen; Hippolytus; Athanasius; Didymus; Aphraates the Persian; Basil the Great; Epiphanius; Nonnus; ps.-Dionysius Alex.; Eustathius; Chrysostom; Theodoret; Cyril four times; Paulus Bishop of Emesa; Theodorus Mops.; Amphilochius; Severus; Theodorus Heracl.; Basilius Cil.; Cosmas; Damascene in 3 places; 4 other ancient Greek writers; and of the Latins, Ambrose; Novatian; Hilary; Lucifer; Victorinus; Jerome; Cassian; Cassian; Vigilius' Zeno; Marius; Maximus Taur.; Capreolus; Augustine, etc. They are even acknowledged by Lachmann, Tregelles, and Tischendorf. Why then is there not so much as a hint from the Revisers that there is such a mass of counter-evidence against the spurious reading of the favored uncials? Shame! Yes, shame on the learning which comes abroad only to perplex the weak, and to unsettle the doubting, and to mislead the blind! Shame on those occupying themselves with falsifying the inspired Greek text in countless places, and branding with suspicion some of the most precious utterances of the Spirit!

---

¹ Let the Reader, with a map spread before him, survey the whereabouts of the several VERSIONS above enumerated, and mentally assign each FATHER to his own approximate locality: then let him bear in mind that 995 out of 1000 of the extant MANUSCRIPTS agree with those Fathers and Versions; and let him further recognize that those MSS. (executed at different dates in different countries) must severally represent independent remote originals, inasmuch as *no two of them are found to be quite alike.*

—Next, let him consider that, *in all the Churches of the East*, these words from the earliest period were read as *part of the Gospel for the Thursday in Easter week.*—This done, let him decide whether it is reasonable that two worshippers of codex B—A.D. 1881—should attempt to thrust all this mass of ancient evidence clean out of sight by their peremptory sentence of exclusion,—' WESTERN AND SYRIAN.'

Drs. Westcott and Hort inform us that '*the character of the attestation* marks' the clause (ὁ ὣν ἐν τῷ οὐρανῷ), 'as a WESTERN GLOSS.' But the 'attestation' for retaining that clause—(*a*) Comes demonstrably from every quarter of ancient Christendom :—(*b*) Is more ancient (by 200 years) than the evidence for omitting it :—(*c*) Is more numerous, in the proportion of 99 to 1:—(*d*) In point of respectability, stands absolutely alone. For since we have *proved* that Origen and Didymus, Epiphanius and Cyril, Ambrose and Jerome, *recognize* the words in dispute, of what possible Textual significancy can it be if presently (*because it is sufficient for their purpose*) the same Fathers are observed to quote S. John iii. 13 *no further than down to the words ' Son of Man*'? No person, (least of all a professed Critic,) who adds to his learning a few grains of common sense and a little candour, can be misled by such a circumstance. Origen, Eusebius, Proclus, Ephraim Syrus, Jerome, Marius, when they are only insisting on the doctrinal significancy of the earlier words, naturally end their quotation at this place. The two Gregories (Naz. [ii. 87, 168]: Nyss. [Galland. vi. 522]), writing against the Apolinarian heresy, of course quoted the verse no further than Apolinaris himself was accustomed (for his heresy) to adduce it. . . . About the *internal* evidence for the clause, nothing has been said; but *this* is simply overwhelming. We make our appeal to *Catholic Antiquity*; and are content to rest our cause on *External Evidence* ;—on COPIES, on VERSIONS, on FATHERS.

No thoughtful person will rise from a discussion like the foregoing without inferring from the facts which have emerged showing the exceeding antiquity of depravations of the inspired Word. It should not be supposed that the present depravation was the work of Apolinarius. Like the rest it is probably older by at least 150 years. Apolinarius, in whose person the heresy which bears his name came to a head, did but inherit the tenets of his predecessors in error. And these had already in various ways resulted in the corruption of the Deposit.

Luke 9:54-56 CORRUPTED BY THE ORTHODOX

There is a singular consent among the Critics for eliminating from S. Luke 9:54-56 twenty-four words which embody two memorable sayings of the Son of Man: *"Lord, wilt Thou that we command fire to come down from Heaven and consume them, [(1) as Elijah did?] But He turned and rebuked them, [(2) and said, You know not what manner of spirit you are of]. [(3) For the Son of Man has not come to destroy men's lives, but to save them.]. And they went to another village. "*The three bracketed clauses contain the twenty-four words in dispute.

The first of these clauses (ὡς καὶ 'Ηλίας ἐποίησε)was rejected by Mill as an obvious interpolation. Griesbach retained it as probably genuine. The second clause (καὶ εἶπεν, οὐκ οἴου πνεύματός ἐστε ὑμεῖς) was obelized by Griesbach as probably not genuine. The third clause (ὁ γὰρ υἱὸς τοῦ ἀνθρώπου οὐκ ἦλθε ψυχὰς ἀνθρώπων ἀπολέσαι, ἀλλὰ σῶσαι)he rejected entirely. Lachmann also retains the first clause, but rejects the other two. Alford, not without misgiving, does the same. Westcott and Hort, without any misgiving about the third clause, are "morally certain" that the first and second clauses are a 'Western interpolation.' Tischendorf and Tregelles are thorough, agreeing in rejecting unceremoniously all the three clauses, as do the Revisers of 1881.

Now it may as well be declared at once that Codd. אBΞ,1,g (1), Cyril,[6]two MSS. of the Bohairic (d 3, d 2), the Lewis and two cursives (71, 157) are literally the only authority, ancient or modern, for so exhibiting the text (bare of the three clauses). Against them are arrayed the whole body of MSS. uncial and cursive, including ACD, every known lectionary, all the Latin and Syriac versions — besides seven good Greek Fathers beginning with Clemens Alex. (A.D. 190), and five Latin Fathers beginning with Tertullian (A.D. 190) — Cyprian's testimony is in fact the voice of the Fourth Council of Carthage (A.D. 253). If on a survey of this body of evidence anyone will gravely tell me that the preponderance of authority still seems to him to be in favor of the shorter reading, I can but suggest that the sooner he communicates to the world the grounds of his opinion, the better.

First, it becomes necessary to consider the disputed clauses separately. This is because ancient authorities, rivaling modern critics, are unable to agree as to which they will reject, which they will retain.

Considering the second clause first, what persuades so many critics to omit the precious words, *'and said, You know not what manner of spirit you are of'* is the discovery that these words are absent from many uncial MSS. — אBAC and nine others — besides, as might have been confidently anticipated from that fact, the words are also missing from a fair proporiton of the cursive copies. It is impossible to deny that on the face of it such an amount of evidence against any words of Scripture is exceedingly weighty. Pseudo-Basil (ii. 271) is found to have read the passage in the same curt way. Cyril, on the other hand, seems to have read it differently.

And yet the entire aspect of the case becomes changed the instant it is perceived that this disputed clause is recognized by Clemens (A.D. 190); as well as by the Old Latin, the Peshitto and the Curetonian Syriac versions — thus establishing the fact that in Eastern as well as in Western Christendom the words under discussion were actually recognized as genuine a hundred and fifty years before the oldest of the extant uncials came into existence. When it is further found that the Vulgate, the Old Egyptian, the Harkleian, the Syriac, and the Gothic versions also contain the words in question — and that Ambrose, Jerome and Augustine recognize them; as well as Chrysostom in four places, Didymus, Epiphanius, Cyril and Theodoret, besides Antiochus familiarly quote them, it is evident that the testimony of antiquity in their favor is even overwhelming. Add that in eight uncial MSS beginning with D, the words in dispute form part of the text of S. Luke, and that they are recognized by the great mass of the cursive copies — only six of the twenty collated by Scrivener being without them — and it is plain that at least five tests of genuineness have been fully satisfied.

Secondly, the third clause, *"For the Son of Man has not come to destroy men's lives, but to save them"* rests on precisely the same solid evidence as the second clause; except that the testimony of Clemens is no longer available because his quotation does not extend so far. Cod. D also omits this third clause. On the other hand it is upheld by Tertullian, Cyprian and Ambrose. Tischendorf suggests that it has surreptitiously found its way into the text from Luke 19:10, or Matt. 19:11 (in which the words ζητῆσαι καὶ do not occur). But this is impossible because what is found in those two is essentially different.

Thirdly, Here we may note how apt an illustration is afforded of the amount of consensus which subsists between documents of the oldest class. This divergence becomes most conspicuous when we direct our attention to the grounds for omitting the first clause, *"as Elijah did"* — for here we discover that the evidence is not only less weighty, but also different. Codexes **B** and ℵ are now forsaken by all their former allies except LΞ and a single cursive copy. True, they are supported by the Curetonian Syriac, the Vulgate, and two copies of the Old Latin. But this time they find themselves confronted by Codexes ACD with thirteen other uncials and the whole body of the cursives; the Peshitto, Coptic, Gothic, and Harkleian versions; by Clemens, Jerome, Chrysostom, Cyril and ps.-Basil. In respect of antiquity, variety, respectability, numbers, they are therefore hopelessly outvoted on this first clause.

HOW HAS ALL THIS DEPRAVITY OF COD. ℵBAC(D)OCCURRED?

It was the favorite tenet with the Gnostic heretics that the Law and the Gospel are at variance. To establish this Marcion (in a work called Antitheses) set passages of the New Testament against passages of the Old — and his followers were taught from the seeming disagreement between the two Testaments that they were to infer that the Law and the Gospel cannot have proceeded from one and the same author. Here was a place exactly suited to Marcion's purpose. The God of the Old Testament had twice sent down fire from Heaven to consume fifty men. But our Saviour said that the Son of Man did not come to destroy men's lives, but to save them. Accordingly, Tertullian in his fourth book against Marcion, refuting his teaching, acquaints us that one of Marcion's 'Contrasts' was Elijah's severity in calling down fire from Heaven — and the gentleness of Christ. Tertullian replies; "I acknowledge the severity of the judge, but I recognize the same severity on the part of Christ towards His Disciples when they proposed to bring down a similar calamity on a Samaritan village." From all of which it is plain that within seventy years of the time when the Gospel was published, the text of S. Luke 9:54-56 stood very much as at present.

But then it is further discovered that at the same remote period (about A.D. 130) this place of Scripture was much fastened on by the enemies of the Gospel. The Manichaean heretics pressed believers with it. The disciples' appeal to the example of Elijah, and the reproof they incurred, became inconvenient facts. The consequence might have been foreseen. With 'commendable' solicitude for God's honor, but through mistaken piety, certain of the orthodox (without suspecting the evil they were committing) were so ill-advised as to erase from their copies the twenty-four words which had been turned to mischievous account, as well as to cause copies to be made of the books so mutilated. And, behold! At the end of 1,700 years there is this calamitous result!

Of these three clauses, then, which are closely inter-dependent, and as Tischendorf admits, all three must stand or all three fall together:

Clause 1 is found with ACD, the Old Latin, the Peshitto, Clement, Chrysostom, Cyril, Jerome — but not with אB, the Vulgate or Curetonian. The second and third clauses are found with the Old Latin, Vulgate, Peshitto, Harkleian, six Greek and five Latin Fathers — but not with אBACD. Only א and B refuse to recognize either the first, second or third clause. And this is a fair sample of that 'singular agreement' which is sometimes said to subsist between 'the lesser group of witnesses.' Is it not plain on the contrary that at a very remote period there existed a fierce conflict, and consequent divergence of testimony about the present passage; of which 1,700 years have failed to obliterate the traces? Had אB been our only ancient guides, it might of course have been contended that there has been no act of spoliation committed. But seeing that one half of the missing treasure is found with their allies ACD, Clement Alex., Chrysostom, Cyril, Jerome — and the other half with their allies, Old Latin, Harkleian, Clement, Tertullian, Cyprian, Ambrose, Didymus, Epiphanius, Chrysostom, Cyril, Theodoret, Jerome, Augustine — it is clear that no such pretence can any longer be set up.

CHAPTER 14 FOOTNOTES

Page 90: ¹When Cyril writes (Scolia, ed. Pusey, vol. vi. 568), "Τὸ δέ παιδίον ηὔξανε καὶ ἐκραταιοῦτο ΠΝΕΥΜΑΤΙΚΑ, πληρούμενον ΣΟΦΙΑ καὶ ΧΑΡΙΤΙ." καίτοι κατά φύσιν παντίλειός ἐστιν ὡς Θεός καὶ ἐξ ἰδίου πληρώματος διανέμει τοῖς ἁγίος τά ΠΝΕΥΜΑΤΙΚΑ, καὶ αὐτός ἐστιν ἡ ΣΟΦΙΑ, καὶ τῆς ΧΑΡΙΤΟΣ ὁ δοτήρ — it is clear that πνεύματι must have stood in Cyril's texte. The same is the reading of Cyril's treatise, De Incarnatione (Mai, ii. 57); and of his Commentary on Luke (ibid. p. 136). One is surprised at Tischendorf's perverse inference concerning the last-named place. Cyril had begun by quoting *the whole of verese 40 in exact conformity with the traditional text* (Mai, ii. 136). At the close of some remarks Cyril proceeds as follows, according to Cramer's Catena: ὁ Εὐαγγελιστής ἔφη "ηὔξανε καὶ ἐκραταιοῦτο" ΚΑΙ ΤΑ ΕΞΗΣ. Surely this constitutes no ground for supposing that he did not recognize the word πνεύματι, but rather that he did. On the other hand, it is undeniable that in V.P. ii. 138 and 139 (Conciia iii. 241 d, 244 a), from Pusey's account of what he found in the MSS. the word πνεύματι must be suspected of being an unauthorized addition to the text of Cyril's treatise, De Recta fide ad Pulcheriam et Eudociam (vii. P. i 277-8).

Page 96: ²IV. 83, 430. But both Origen (i. 705; iv. 320, 402) and Cyril (iv. 554; v. 758) quote the traditional reading; and Cyril (iv. 549) distinctly says that the latter is right, and παρά τοῦ πατρός wrong.

Page 96: ³Excerpt. Theod. 968 — Heracleon's name is also connected by Origen with this text. Valentinus (*ap*. Iren. 100) says, ὅν δή καὶ υἱόν Μονογενῆ καὶ Θεόν κέκληκεν.

Page 97: ⁴The Gnostics Basilides and Valentinus were the direct precursors of Apolonius, Photinus, Nestorius, etc., in assailing the doctrine of the Incarnation. Their heresy must have been actively at work when S. John wrote his first (4:1,2,3) and second (verse 7) Epistles.

Page 97: ⁵Chrysostom wrote: Ἐπιπηδῶσιν ἡμῖν οἱ αἱρετικοὶ λέγοντες ἰδοὺ οὐκ ἀνέλαβε σάρκα ὁ Χριστός ὁ δεύτ. γάρ φησιν ἄνθρ. ὁ κ. ἐξ οὐρανοῦ (Chrys. iii. 114 b.).

Page 101: ⁶The text of S. Luke 9:51-56 prefixed to Cyril's fifty-sixth sermon (p 253) is the text of B and א — an important testimony to what I suppose may be regarded as the Alexandrine *Textus Receptus* of this place in the fifth century. But then no one supposes that Cyril is individually responsible for the headings on his sermons. We therefore refer to the body of his discourse, and there we discover that the Syriac translator as as usual rendered it with exceeding licence. He has omitted to render some such words as the following which certainly stood in the original text: εἰδέναι γάρ χρή, ὅτι ὡς μήπω τῆς νέας κεκρατηκότες χάριτος, ἀλλ' ἔτι τῆς προτέρας ἐχόμενοι συνηθείας, τοῦτο εἶπον, πρὸς Ἡλίαν ἀφορῶντες τὸν πυρί καταφλέξαντα δὶς τοὺς πεντήκοντα καὶ τοὺς ἡγουμένους αὐτῶν. (Cramer's Cat. ii. p. 81. Cf. Corderii, Cat. p. 263. Also Matthaei. N.T. *in loc*., pp. 223-4) Now the man who wrote *that*, must surely have read S. Luke 9:54, 55 as we do.

Made in the USA
Lexington, KY
13 June 2018